THE UNIVERSITY

User Centred Design

D1494728

London: The Stationery Office

CCTA
Central Computer and Telecommunications Agency

Published with the permission of the Central Computer and Telecommunications Agency on behalf of the Controller of Her Majesty's Stationery Office.

First published 2000

ISBN 0 11 330873 6

Titles within the Business Systems Development series include:

SSADM Foundation	ISBN 0 11 330870 1
Data Modelling	ISBN 0 11 330871 X
The Business Context	ISBN 0 11 330872 8
User Centred Design	ISBN 0 11 330873 6
Behaviour and Process Modelling	ISBN 0 11 330874 4
Function Modelling	ISBN 0 11 330875 2
Database and Physical Process Design	ISBN 0 11 330876 0
Also available as a boxed set	ISBN 0 11 330883 3

For further information on CCTA products
Contact:

CCTA Help Desk
Rosebery Court
St Andrews Business Park
Norwich NR7 0HS
Tel 01603 704567 GTN 3040 4567   20625855

CONTENTS

FOREWORD

The Business Systems Development (BSD) series represents 'best practice' approaches to investigating, modelling and specifying Information Systems. The techniques described within this series have been used on systems development projects for a number of years and a substantial amount of experience has contributed to the development of this guidance.

Within the BSD series the techniques are organised into groups that cover specific areas of the development process, for example *User Centred Design* which covers all aspects of the investigation, specification and design of the user interface.

The techniques provide a practical approach to the analysis and design of IT systems. They can also be used in conjunction with other complementary techniques such as Object-Oriented techniques.

The material used within this series originated in the Structured Systems Analysis and Design Method (SSADM) which was introduced by the CCTA as a standard method for the development of medium to large IT systems. Since its introduction in the early 1980's, SSADM has been developed through a number of versions to keep pace with the evolving technology and approaches in the IT industry.

The *SSADM Foundation* volume within the BSD series describes the basic concepts of the method and the way in which it can be employed on projects. It also describes how the different techniques can be used in combination. Each of the other volumes in the series describes techniques and approaches for developing elements of the overall specification and design. These can be used in conjunction with one another or as part of alternative approaches. Cross-referencing is provided in outline within the description of each of the techniques to give pointers to the other approaches and techniques that should be considered for use in combination with the one being described.

All volumes within the Business System Development series are available from:

The Stationery Office
St Crispins
Duke Street
Norwich
NR3 1PD

Acknowledgments

Laurence Slater of Slater Consulting Ltd is acknowledged for editing existing material and where necessary developing new material for the volumes within the Business Systems Development series. John Hall, Jennifer Stapleton, Caroline Slater and Ian Clowes are acknowledged for much of the original material on which this series is based.

The following are thanked for their contribution and co-operation in the development of this series:

Paul Turner	-	Parity Training
Tony Jenkins	-	Parity Training
Caroline Slater	-	Slater Consulting Ltd

In addition to those named above a number of people agreed to review aspects of the series and they are thanked accordingly.

1 INTRODUCTION AND OVERALL CONCEPTS FOR USER CENTRED DESIGN

This volume is concerned with the design of the new system from the user's perspective. It includes techniques that can be used as part of investigation to gather details of the way the users are organised within the business and others that can be used as part of the specification of the new system to document the way the new system will look from the user's perspective.

The ultimate aim of this part of the development lifecycle is to define the on-line IT processes that the system will need to implement and to define the user interface necessary to support these processes. In a traditional development the outputs from Function Definition provide the first area whilst the outputs from User Interface Design provide the second. As the tools for incremental development have increased over recent years so has the idea that a system can be developed incrementally using prototyping techniques as the main driver. The advent of new technologies (e.g., e-commerce and electronic mail) have made this method of development more prevalent as it is seen that this way of working produces systems more quickly. Even in these systems it is important that the system built is the correct one and that the interface is a 'friendly' one. To achieve this it is necessary that some formality must be brought to the prototyping.

Five techniques are covered within this volume. These are:

- **Work Practice Modelling**, which examines the way the users are organised within the business and maps them to the Business Activity Model in order to identify tasks;

- **User Object Modelling**, which develops a model of the way the user views the new system in terms of the business processes, the information to be used by the business and the way in which it will be processed;

- **Function Definition**, which defines the processing that will be required to be automated in the new system for the on-line parts of the system;

- **User Interface Design**, which defines the windows which the user will require to use to access and modify the data within the new system. It also defines the way the individual windows will be navigated;

- **Prototyping and Evaluation**, in which views of the new system are developed which can be demonstrated to the users so that basic requirements and features can be discussed with the users. Some prototypes are used as part of the incremental development of the system.

Figure 1-1 shows the relationships between the individual techniques.

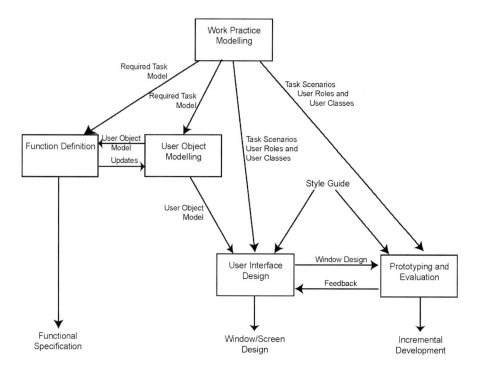

Figure 1-1 Relationship between individual techniques

How many of the techniques a project uses and the tailoring of them will depend upon the depth of analysis and design the project wishes to go to. Obviously if screen design is the only desired aim of User Centred Design then User Interface Design is the minimum and if an incremental build is the aim then Prototyping and Evaluation is the minimum. Factors that might influence the choice of techniques within User Centred Design are:

- length of development time available to the team;

- size of new system;

- how much the design of the system is embedded in the way the users work;

- how much scope there is for changing the user's organisation.

Each project must tailor User Centred Design to suit its own circumstances.

In this series all products are shown in the context of the System Development Template (SDT). This is a template which divides the system development process into activity areas onto which the development products may be mapped. Annexe A provides a fuller description of the System Development Template. Figure 1-2 shows how the products of User Centred Design fit into the System Development Template.

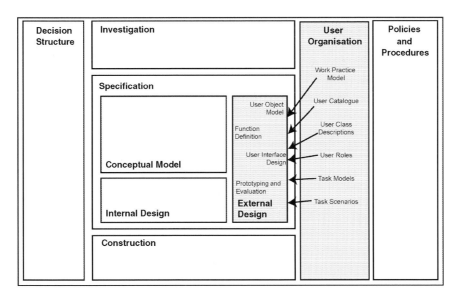

Figure 1-2 Place of User Centred Design products in the System Development Template

Organisation of this volume

After this (introductory) chapter the following is the organisation for this volume.

Chapter 2 – Work Practice Modelling. This is a full description of the concepts, products and techniques necessary to produce the Work Practice Model.

Chapter 3 – User Object Modelling. This is a full description of the concepts, products and techniques necessary to produce the User Object Model.

Chapter 4 – Function Definition. This is a full description of the concepts, products and techniques necessary to produce the Function Definitions.

Chapter 5 – User Interface Design. This is a full description of the concepts, products and techniques necessary to produce the Window/Screen Design.

Chapter 6 – Prototyping and Evaluation. This is a full description of the concepts, products and techniques necessary to develop prototypes that can be shown to the user and then the methods for evaluating the results of prototyping.

Chapter 7 – Meta-model. To assist projects and CASE tool developers, a Meta-model is provided which shows the basic concepts covered in this volume and way they inter-relate.

Chapter 8 – Product Descriptions. Product descriptions are provided for all the major products described in this volume. These should be used by projects as a basis for the product descriptions to be used on the project. (Note: It is expected that the project will need to tailor these product descriptions so that items not required are omitted and any other items required by the project included.)

Annexes. There are three annexes appended to this volume. The first gives a description of the System Development Template, the second is a description of EU-Rent which is the case study that is used throughout this volume. The third is a glossary of terms that are relevant to this volume.

2   WORK PRACTICE MODELLING

2.1   Work Practice Modelling

Projects are likely to run into trouble if they develop a new automated system without first considering – and possibly changing – the way in which the business is organised in terms of the business activities undertaken and the tasks undertaken by people and computers within the business environment. Computer-based systems have a major role to play in the way people perform their day-to-day tasks.

The activities of Business Activity Modelling[1] give the analyst the opportunity to re-think the business activities whilst Work Practice Modelling takes this further by outlining who does what and where within the new system, based on the business activities identified and the proposed user organisation.

Work Practice Modelling products are within the User Organisation area of the System Development Template as shown in Figure 2-1.

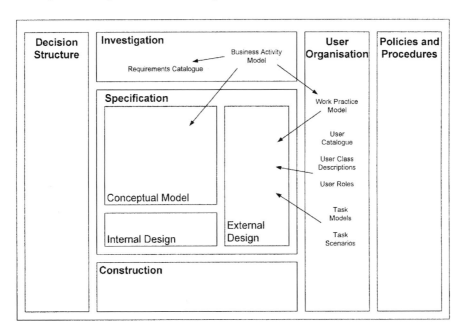

Figure 2-1 Work Practice Modelling products in the System Development Template

Projects require an approach for the following:

---

[1] See *The Business Context* in this series for a full description of the concepts, products and techniques of Business Activity Modelling.

- allocating responsibilities for business activity to organisational units;

- defining tasks for people within the organisational units;

- assembling job specifications from tasks;

- creating interfaces between user tasks and the automated system.

The Work Practice Model is a mapping of the Business Activity Model onto the 'actors' within the Organisation Structure specified for the business area in which the new system will reside. This is developed using a number of different techniques/products:

- **User Analysis** studies the characteristics of potential users of the new automated system and defines user roles;

- **Task Modelling** builds on the definition of who does what in the Work Practice Model and defines in more detail the tasks they will perform, taking into account the user characteristics defined in User Analysis;

- **Task Scenarios** are descriptions of specific examples of tasks based on situations that are likely to occur. These are used initially to validate and enhance the results of Task Modelling and later as a basis for prototyping and testing.

A variety of techniques may be used in order to map the user Organisation onto the Business Activity Model. There is no single approach advocated by this volume. There are several reasons for this:

- the approach will depend, to a large extent, on the approach chosen for Business Activity Modelling;

- each Organisation will have its own split of responsibilities between IT practitioners and Human Factors specialists;

- some organisations may already have selected techniques to model Work Practice, particularly in the area of job design.

The overriding consideration in the approach adopted for Work Practice Modelling is that projects should take account of the complete picture of the business and not just concentrate on the automated system. The automated system must be designed to fit the business needs, not the other way round.

This chapter simply describes the basic areas that should be covered by Work Practice Modelling and describes the types of products that may be produced.

The relationship between the Business Activity Model and the Work Practice Model

The Business Activity Modelling chapter (see *The Business Context* volume in this series) emphasises the need for a Business Activity Model that defines business activities in terms of:

- why the Organisation is doing what it is doing – the business perspectives;

- what the Organisation is doing – business activities and the dependencies between them;

- when activities are done – business events and the activities they trigger;

- how activities are done – business rules, defining constraints and operational guidance for activities.

The Work Practice Model is a mapping of the Business Activity Model onto an Organisation (management structure, actors, geography), to specify:

- who (which actors) actually carries out each business activity;

- where the activities are carried out.

If the Organisation is restructured but the business remains the same, it should be necessary to change only the Work Practice Model and the External Design – the Business Activity Model and requirements for IT support of the Business Activity Model should remain unchanged by changes to the Organisation.

Overview of Work Practice Modelling

The relationship of Work Practice Modelling products with other system development products is shown in Figure 2-2.

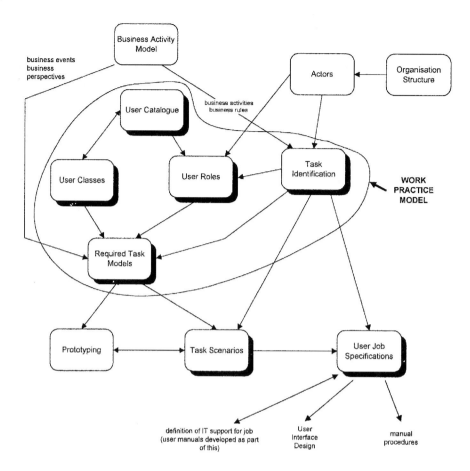

Figure 2-2 Context of Work Practice Modelling

The components shown in shadowed boxes on the diagram are described further in this chapter. The components shown without shadowing are described as follows:

- **Business Activity Model**. This describes the essential business activities that need to be undertaken in this area of the business, and the business events that trigger activities. The Business Activity Model does not indicate the Organisation Structure or 'who does what';

- **Organisation Structure**. This identifies broad areas of responsibility and will contain all the actors of the business system. When mapped onto the Business Activity Model, it is possible to identify which actors will perform each of the business activities. Generally the Organisation Structure may be fixed, in which case it is a constraint on the Work Practice Model. Alternatively, a development project may be permitted to make proposals for changing the Organisation Structure;

- **Actors**. Actors are the business roles that people adopt within the Organisation Structure. Actors perform business activities – this cross-reference is established in

Work Practice Modelling. Actors may become user roles when the boundary of the automated system is set.

- **Prototyping**. Prototyping is useful in support of the development of job designs which involve the on-line use of the automated system. This subject area is described in more detail in the Prototyping and Evaluation chapter (see Chapter 6).

An overview of the sequence of activities within a project is shown in Figure 2-3.

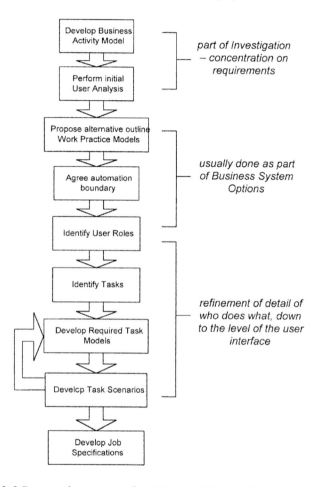

Figure 2-3 Proposed sequence of activities within a project

The sequence of activities chosen for a specific project will depend upon the techniques chosen for Business Activity Modelling and task identification.

The activities shown in Figure 2-3 are described in more detail as follows:

- **Develop Business Activity Model**. This is where the essential business activities, business perspectives, business events and business rules are defined with no constraints of user Organisation or geography (see *The Business Context* volume in this series);

- **Perform initial User Analysis**. Here the initial User Catalogue is started based upon the users of the current system. User Analysis cannot be completed until the automation boundary is decided – at this point the full user population will be known;

- **Propose alternative outline Work Practice Models**. The Business Activity Model could be mapped onto the User Organisation and geography in a number of different ways. There may be scope for changing the User Organisation to achieve optimum allocation of business activities to actors. An outline Organisation Structure and allocation of business activities to actors needs to be developed as a basis for the identification of tasks and the design of jobs;

- **Agree automation boundary**. The Business Activity Model and outline Work Practice Model, together with the Requirements Catalogue, can be used to agree the boundary of the automated system;

- **Identify User Roles**. Once the automation boundary has been agreed, user roles can be derived with reference to the needs of actors to access the same areas of functionality with the same levels of authority;

- **Identify Tasks** and **Develop Required Task Models**. Tasks are identified as sets of business activities undertaken by an actor or user role in response to a business event. Each task can be broken down into sub-tasks to an appropriate level where the precise allocation of responsibilities between human and automated system can be defined and agreed. Tasks and Required Task Models concentrate on the human activities required to respond to the business event – functions are used to define the automated support for the tasks (see Chapter 3);

- **Develop Task Scenarios**. Scenarios covering the major and critical areas of the business are devised for individual tasks. The scenarios illustrate real-life situations to help validate the Required Task Models and to act as the basis for prototyping;

- **Develop Job Specifications**. The tasks for specific actors and user roles are pulled together into coherent job specifications that can be given to individuals. These will detail how combinations of tasks are allocated and what is required to meet the objectives of the business.

2.2   Concepts of Work Practice Modelling

This chapter describes the products of Work Practice Modelling. In order to construct these products, it is important to understand some of the basic concepts. These have been introduced above but are summarised briefly here and expanded throughout the chapter.

2.2.1 Actor

Actors can be identified as a collection of proposed job holders who will share a large proportion of common tasks, whether using the IT system or not. Actors will often be identified by defining coherent sets of business activities which will be performed by the same people.

2.2.2 Basic task

The complete set of business activities triggered by a single business event irrespective of who or what is to perform the business activities.

2.2.3 Business event

A business event is a trigger to one or more business activities. Business events are defined as part of the Business Activity Model. Each business event is of one of three types:

- external inputs – inputs from outside the business system boundary;
- decisions made internally to the business system;
- scheduled points in time.

The set of business activities triggered by a business event is defined as a basic task. The portion of a basic task undertaken by a single actor or user role is defined as a task. Where more than one actor and/or user role is required to undertake business activities in response to a business event, it follows that a single business event can initiate more than one task.

2.2.4 Task

A task is a human activity performed by an actor or user role in response to a business event. The task is identified with reference to all the business activities triggered by a specific business event which are undertaken by a single actor or user role.

It should be stressed that tasks are identified from the 'human' perspective. Many tasks will not involve direct interaction with the automated system. Within a single task there may be some sub-tasks that require interaction with the automated system and other sub-tasks that do not. Tasks that require interaction with the automated system are used to derive the User Object Model (see Chapter 3) and Function Definitions (see Chapter 4).

The totality of tasks for a particular actor will form the basis of the job specification for that actor.

2.2.5 Task Scenario

A Task Scenario is a concrete example of a specific task which provides a complete story.

2.2.6 User

A user is a person who will require direct interaction with the automated system.

2.2.7 User role

User roles are derived with reference to actors – they are the subset of actors who require a user interface to the automated system. User roles might be organised slightly differently from actors as they can be defined as groups of users who will require access to the same sets of functions with the same level of authority. Required Task Models can be constructed for actors who have no involvement in the use of the system. Where user roles have been defined, the Required Task Models will be for user roles.

2.2.8 User class

A user class is a subset of the total population of users of the required system who are similar in terms of their frequency of use, relevant knowledge and personal experience. A user class is a category of users who have similar personal characteristics and capabilities. These characteristics and capabilities will help to determine aspects of the style of the user interface. Where more than one user class is identified in a population of users, the user interface will usually be designed to be usable by all classes. In extreme cases, different styles of interaction may be designed for use by different user classes.

2.3   Products of Work Practice Modelling

Some products covered by the technique of Work Practice Modelling are not described in detail here but will be required as a prerequisite to the products described in detail in this chapter. The less detailed products cover the mapping of business activities from the Business Activity Model onto the actors defined as part of the Organisation Structure for the new business system. These products cannot be defined in terms of form or syntax as they will be dependent upon the technique/method selected for performing Business Activity Modelling. However, they should be regarded as of key importance in the development of the Work Practice Model as they will drive the derivation of all other products described here.

The products covered in detail by this chapter are as follows:

- **Required Task Models**. The complete set of Required Task Models describes all of the human activities and task sequences required by the business system. The Required Task Models elaborate the tasks identified by the mapping of business activities onto the user organisation. Required Task Models cover all of the main task areas and some of the less common tasks. A single Required Task Model consists of the following:
    - **Task Model Structure**. A diagrammatic structure of a single task and its sub-tasks;

- ▪ **Task Descriptions**. Task Descriptions are the supporting documentation for the Task Models. They are textual descriptions of each task.

- **Task Scenarios**. A Task Scenario is a concrete example of a specific task which provides a complete story. A Task Scenario describes the actions that the user will perform in using the system to achieve some goal or respond to an event. Task Scenarios are used to validate the Required Task Model and can be used as the basis for prototyping and testing;

- **User Catalogue**. The User Catalogue is a list of all members of the organisation within which the new system will be implemented and who are likely to require access to the new system. The catalogue will describe the tasks associated with each user. It is used as input to the identification of user roles;

- **User Class Descriptions**. A User Class Description is an optional product used where it is considered important to classify users in terms of their relevant knowledge and personal experience;

- **User roles**. User roles are those actors or groups of actors who will require access to the same facilities of the automated system who also have the same level of authority/ responsibility or security level within the Organisation. They are defined in order to develop a single interface for all users who have the same requirements to access system functions.

These products will be described in more detail in the following paragraphs.

2.3.1 Required Task Model

A Required Task Model is a hierarchical model of a task. It consists of a Task Model Structure and one or more Task Descriptions (see Figure 2-4). At the top level, a task is identified as a set of business activities undertaken by a single actor or user role in response to a business event; for example, dealing with walk-in rentals, or recording new bookings for cars.

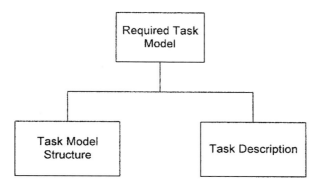

Figure 2-4 Task Model composition

2.3.2 Task Model Structure

A Task Model Structure represents a task and its sub-tasks by a hierarchy. A variety of different notations can be used for this type of structure one of which is shown in Figure 2-5.

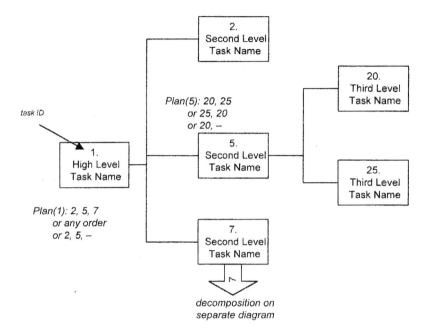

Figure 2-5 Structure conventions for Task Model Structure

All the boxes on the diagram are 'hard boxes'. The top box of the structure contains the name of the overall task.

The basic structure contains the following components:

- boxes which represent tasks or sub-tasks;

- lines which indicate decomposition. Note, there is no sequence, selection or iteration implied in the diagram – this is provided by the plan (see next bullet);

- the possible sequences of sub-tasks within a task or superior sub-task are described in a 'plan' which is placed on the diagram as free text near to the task or sub-task to which it applies;

- boxes which are decomposed on another diagram are indicated by a thick arrow containing the identifier of the other diagram;

- tasks have task identifiers which can be numeric. Every task or sub-task is uniquely identified – this allows sub-tasks to be re-used in a number of different task hierarchies.

An example Task Model Structure for the task 'Walk-in Rental' from the EU-Rent system is shown in Figure 2-6; Figure 2-7 and Figure 2-8 are lower level expansions of two of the sub-tasks in the main diagram.

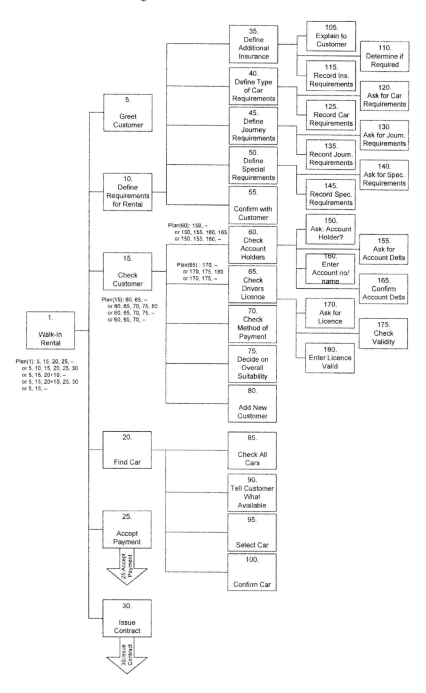

Figure 2-6 Example Task Model Structure for tasks dealing with 'Walk-in Rentals'

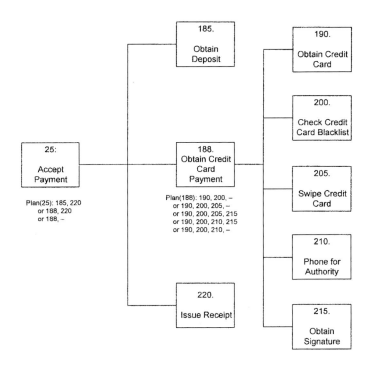

Figure 2-7 Task Model Structure for sub-task 'Accept Payment'

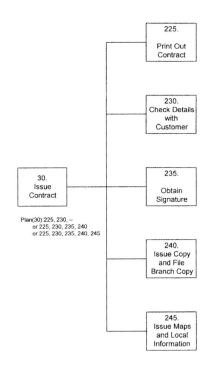

Figure 2-8 Task Model Structure for sub-task 'Issue Contract'

Within the 'Walk-in Rentals' task, there are sub-tasks that will be used in other tasks, for example:

- 10 and l5 will be used in the 'Accept Advanced Booking' task;

- 25 and 30 will be used in the task to support the customer picking up a car that has been booked in advance;

- 30 will also be used when the customer returns the car after renting it if the booking has been extended.

Note that the plans help to avoid the basic structure becoming too complicated.

It may be considered beneficial to use a notation other than the one demonstrated above:

- if a particular notation has been chosen to develop the Business Activity Model, it may be appropriate to use the same or similar notation to extend them to become Task Models Structures;

- where a diagramming tool is not available to construct a Task Model Structure diagram, it may be considered preferable to construct the structure as a simple indented list, possibly with the use of an outlining facility in a word processor. A partial example of the Task Model Structure shown in Figure 2-6 re-expressed as an indented list is shown in Figure 2-9.

```
1: Walk-in Rental
        5.      Greet Customer
        10.     Define Requirements for Rental
                35.     Define Additional Insurance
                        105.    Explain to Customer
                        110.    Determine if Required
                        115.    Record Insurance Requirements
                40.     Define Type of Car Requirements
                45.     Define Journey Requirements
                50.     Define Special Requirements
                55.     Confirm with Customer
        15.     Check Customer
        20.     Find Car
        25.     Accept Payment
        30.     Issue Contract
```

Figure 2-9 Example of a partial Task Model Structure as an indented list

2.3.3 Task Descriptions

A Task Description is completed as background information to any task or sub-task considered to require further description. In general, one Task Description would normally be completed for a whole task. However, where sub-tasks are re-used in other tasks, there is an advantage in completing a Task Description for each of the common sub-tasks in addition to the whole task. Also, if the task is very large, it may be considered more useful to complete Task Descriptions for sub-tasks. A Task Description would rarely be completed for a bottom-level sub-task as this would be at too low a level of detail.

The type of information that may be recorded for a task includes the following:

- triggering business event;
- task goal;
- actor/user role;
- frequency – how often it is performed;
- expected duration of task;
- context of the task;
- physical environment of the task;
- task preconditions;
- equipment used to perform the task;
- information required to perform the task (this is used to help in deriving user objects in the User Object Model – see Chapter 4).

An example Task Description for the task dealing with Walk-in Rentals is shown in Figure 2-10. The relevant Task Model Structure is shown in Figure 2-6.

Task/Sub-Task Name:	1. Walk-in Rental
Business Event:	Customer arrives to rent car without pre-booking
Task goal	To issue a suitable car to the walk-in customer
Actor/User Role	Booking Clerk
Frequency	Different for different branch types: • Airport (small) – 5 per day (medium) – 20 per day (large) – 100 per day • City – 15 per day
Expected duration of task	5 minutes
Context of task	Booking clerk sits at desk, deals with customers requiring walk-in bookings and advanced bookings. Also deals with returns. Actual allocation of car done by system although confirmed with customer for walk-in rentals. Car keys handed to customer by car park supervisor.
Physical environment	Booking clerk sits at desk with terminal, printer, credit card swipe machine and telephone within easy reach. In larger branches, branch manager is in back office – in smaller offices, branch manager may be located at nearby branch.
Task preconditions	None
Information used to perform task	Customer account holders, cars available, car groups and prices, credit card blacklist, conditions of rental, special options available and prices, insurance options, EU-Rent customer blacklist, maps and local guides.

Figure 2-10 Example Task Description

Where sub-tasks are performed under more than one leg of the hierarchy, a (Common) Task Description is completed which is referenced from each of the relevant tasks via the sub-task identifier. An example of a Task Description for the common sub-task 'Check Customer' is shown in Figure 2-11.

Task/Sub-Task Name:	15. Check Customer
Cross-reference to tasks	1. Walk-in Rental 325. Advanced Booking
Business Event:	See owing task
Task/sub-task goal	To determine whether the person is acceptable as an EU-Rent customer
Actor	Booking Clerk
Frequency	Different for different branch types: • Airport (small) – 8 per day (medium) – 30 per day (large) – 120 per day • City – 15 per day
Expected duration of task	1 minute
Context of task	See owing task
Physical environment	See owing task
Task preconditions	Person expresses wish to rent car.
Information used to perform task	Customer account holders, EU-Rent customer blacklist.

Figure 2-11 Example Task Description for common sub-task

2.3.4 Task Scenario

A Task Scenario is a concrete example of a specific path through a task. Each Task Scenario describes the actions that a user will perform in using the system to achieve a goal or respond to a specific example of a business event. It can be written in the form of a story or a script. The Task Scenario is validated with users to gain an understanding of what the system is likely to need to cope with. Task Scenarios can be used for the following purposes:

- to validate subsequent design work;

- to identify tasks that have been missed in the construction of Task Models;

- as an input to prototyping;

- to improve communication with users;

- as the basis of user acceptance testing.

Each Task Scenario consists of a textual description of the scenario including inputs, background and the way in which the tasks are performed. Sub-tasks performed by the system should be distinguished from sub-tasks performed by the user where this split can be identified. It can be written in the form of a story or a script. The scenario should be annotated to indicate whether this is a typical scenario or likely to be an exception.

An example Task Scenario taken from EU-Rent is shown in Figure 2-12.

Task Scenario: Mother with Children – Walk-in Rental	
User Role	Booking Clerk
Frequency	80% of all bookings are for Car Group 1 5% of bookings require child seats
Background	A woman aged 23 with two small children and a baby comes in. She asks for the cheapest car possible for the next three days.
Description	

A woman aged 23 with two small children and a baby comes in. She asks for the cheapest car possible for the next three days. She has an emergency and has to travel only 30 miles but will need a car when she gets there.

The children both require child seats, there must be a safe place for the baby in its pram.

After checking on what is available the clerk says that there is only one cheapest rate car available which is straight out of the showroom.

She turns this down as she is worried about her children making a mess and having to pay a penalty.

The clerk offers her a higher rate but older car at a special rate based on the fact that she is only going to use a low mileage.

She accepts the car. The clerk rings up the garage to get the child seats put in.

The clerk asks for the customer's name and address. The customer tells the clerk who enters the customer's details as she talks.

The clerk asks to see the customer's driving licence. It is clean so the clerk enters the fact in the system.

The clerk creates a new rental which automatically has the customer and car details entered and tells the customer the terms and conditions for insurance.

The customer thinks about the terms and conditions and accepts them.

The clerk asks how the customer will pay the deposit and the final payment on return.

The customer says cash which the clerk enters in the system.

Then she changes her mind and says that she would rather use a cheque for the deposit.

The change is made to the form.

The clerk prints out the contract and asks the customer to sign the top copy as acceptance of the terms and conditions.

The client does this and writes out a cheque and provides the cheque card.

The clerk verifies the signature and marks the rental as agreed between both parties, gives the keys from the rack behind her to the customer and asks the customer to wait until the car is ready.

The clerk puts the signed copy of the rental form in the rental file for the day.

The clerk clears the screen ready for the next customer who is waiting in line.

Figure 2-12 Example Task Scenario

2.3.5 User Catalogue

A User Catalogue is a description of the target users and the task areas they undertake. A User Catalogue can be initiated based on the users of the current system provided there is minimal restructuring anticipated. Its main focus should be on recording details of users and tasks necessary for the required system. The purpose of the User Catalogue is to assist in the identification of user roles from actors.

The User Catalogue will cover the following areas:

- the users in the target population;

- the task areas performed by each of the users.

If the system being designed is very large, covering a large user population, it may be appropriate to document the User Catalogue by actor or business applications rather than by individual user. This means that in some cases individuals will be identified and in other cases only actor names will be identified.

There are no rules of notation or syntax for the User Catalogue. It should be produced in a format most suited to the project environment and tools available. An example of a User Catalogue is shown in Figure 2-13.

User/Actor	Task areas
Maintenance Foreman	Record work done on maintenance work Check car out from maintenance Distribute job sheets to maintenance workers Supervise work done
Branch Manager	Buy and sell cars Supervise Branch Booking Clerks Greet Customer Fill-in for Booking Clerk Deal with Customer queries Explain rejection reasons for failed rental requests Promulgate company policy decisions to all branch staff
Branch Booking Clerk	Greet Customer Accept Rental Request Allocate cars to rentals Give car documents and keys to customer Give contract to customer Make bookings for maintenance or transfer Deal with walk-in rentals

Figure 2-13 Example User Catalogue

From this example, taken from the EU-Rent system, it can be seen that the Branch Manager can be required to 'fill in' for the Booking Clerks – it is this type of overlap between the responsibilities of different actors that will help in the subsequent identification of user roles.

2.3.6 User Class Descriptions

User Class Descriptions are an optional product that would normally only be produced when there is a large and diverse user population. A User Class Description can be used to provide a detailed description of a category of user which is used to determine the requirements for the style and general features of the user interface design. The information that is collected needs to be motivated by the design choices that are being considered.

The categories of information that can be recorded for each class include the following:

- type of user (direct/indirect/remote, etc.);

- experience level – both in the use of user interfaces and in the job (novice, intermediate, expert, etc.);

- frequency of use of the system (one hour a day, once a week, continuous, etc.) and length of time in job;

- whether the user has to use the system to do their job or can choose not to use it (mandatory/discretionary);

- education/intellectual abilities (typical qualifications held by members of the class, abilities required by tasks currently performed);

- motivation for using the system and the specific goals (likely costs/benefits of the new system to this user class, increase/decrease in skills/prestige, etc.);

- numbers of users in the user class;

- training received/required;

- tasks performed (cross-reference to Required Task Models);

- other tools/systems used in performing their jobs.

For each user class it is useful to identify the implications of their characteristics on the user interface that they will require: for example, if a number of users are unable to read English, extensive use of icons may be preferable to menus with text descriptions.

An example User Class Description taken from the EU-Rent system is shown in Figure 2-14.

User class: Dedicated reception desk staff		
User attribute	**Description**	**Implied Usability Requirement**
Type of User	Dedicated	Usability is very important for this class of user
Experience Level	Intermediate – staff have been using a character-based system for part of their work to date – experience of GUI-based systems low	Full user training will be important
Frequency of use of the system	6 hours per day	Performance on common tasks is important
Mandatory/ discretionary	Mandatory	
Education/ intellectual abilities	Most recruited from school with two GCSE A levels as the entry requirement	Users will be able to cope with a relatively complex interface – possible use of shortcuts for efficiency
Motivation for using the system	Skill levels in business knowledge will be decreased – the system will perform some of the decision making performed by the user to date. Job can be performed more efficiently – will give the users a more professional image. Increase general computer skills – first use of GUI.	
Number of users in class	250 for system as a whole, 4 per site	
Training received/ required	All reception staff attend a three-day training course on the system and are supervised for first two weeks of usage.	
Regular tasks	All tasks involving customers who come into branch offices.	
Other tools/systems used	Calculator Diary on wall of scheduled maintenance Word processor	

Figure 2-14 Example User Class Description from the EU-Rent system

2.3.7 User roles

User roles are those actors who will require direct access to the automated system within the business system.

The documentation of the user roles lists the individual roles, the corresponding actors and the tasks associated with them.

There are no rules of syntax or notation for the user role documentation. The precise format will depend upon the project environment and the tools available. From the User Catalogue in Figure 2-13, it is possible to identify three user roles:

- maintenance supervisor;

- branch manager;

- booking clerk.

At first sight these may appear to be the same as the job titles given above. However, the difference is that when the manager 'fills in' for the booking clerk, he/she is adopting the role of booking clerk – this is not part of the branch manager's user role. This is demonstrated in Figure 2-15.

User Role	Actor/User Name	Tasks
Maintenance Supervisor	Maintenance Foreman	Record work done on maintenance Check car out from maintenance Distribute job sheets to maintenance workers Supervise work done
Branch Manager	Branch Manager	Buy and sell cars Supervise Branch Booking Clerks Greet Customer Deal with Customer queries Explain rejection reasons for failed rental requests Promulgate company policy decisions to all branch staff
Booking Clerk	Branch Manager Branch Booking Clerk	Greet Customer Accept Rental Request Allocate cars to rentals Give car documents and keys to customer Give contract to customer Make bookings for maintenance or transfer

Figure 2-15 Example user role documentation

The identification of user roles allows individuals to adopt different roles in different circumstances. This is rationalising users based on their need to access common functions. Conversely, if two sets of users share similar tasks but one set is permitted access to different sets of data from the other, it is necessary to identify different user roles to allow the different access requirements to be highlighted in the design.

2.4   The Work Practice Modelling Technique

Work Practice Modelling covers the following topics:

- mapping the Business Activity Model onto the Organisation;

- user analysis;

- Task Modelling;

- developing prototype designs;

- specifying usability requirements.

The extent to which each of these activities is undertaken within an individual project, and the most appropriate time to do them, will depend upon project circumstances and the skills available. There are several important things to keep in mind:

- the aim is to help develop a design for the entire business system using a combination of systems analysis and human factors skills. It is only when this overall design is understood that systems analysts can start being more specific about identifying the user–computer boundary and defining requirements for the user interface;

- it is not likely to be possible to complete the whole of Work Practice Modelling before any specification and design are started – this is an iterative process which will start with an initial view that is subsequently refined as the project proceeds. It is important not to spend too long in refining early views before moving on to other activities;

- developers need direct contact with users throughout so they can understand their perspectives and how they are likely to need to use the system. This prevents analysts from using themselves as examples of typical users;

- the differences between classes of users are only relevant inasmuch as they will affect the design of the user interface – there is no point in spending a lot of time documenting characteristics which will have no effect on the way the user interface is designed and implemented;

- a glossary of user terminology is an extremely useful document that can be used to ensure that user terms are properly understood by the analysts. This is particularly important where users understand something specific by terms used in general computer jargon, for example, 'clear' might be used as a term to clear the screen in a computer system but to air-traffic controllers it means that a plane is able to take off. The glossary can be used to ensure that the final user interface contains terms which have meanings understood by users.

The different areas covered by Work Practice Modelling are described in more detail in the following paragraphs.

2.4.1 Mapping the Business Activity Model onto the Organisation

The mapping of the Business Activity Model onto the User Organisation can be undertaken using the following activities as a guide:

- define Organisation Structure and actors; specify basic tasks;

- specify interactions between tasks;

- allocate tasks to actors;

- specify interactions between actors and the IT system and identify user roles;

- allocate actors to job specifications.

This set of activities allocates tasks to actors in the business system and makes some initial decisions about where the interface between people and computer will be. This will produce the outline Work Practice Model. Following this, or in parallel, User Analysis can be undertaken to define the user population more clearly so that the Required Task Models can be developed, Task Scenarios for the new system can be devised and individual jobs can be designed.

The development of an outline Work Practice Model is described in more detail in the following paragraphs. Please note that these activities are not meant to be taken as prescriptive. They are given as an example of the types of activity that will need to be undertaken in this area. Specific methods or techniques in this area may vary from project to project and will be dependent upon the techniques chosen for Business Activity Modelling.

Define the Organisation Structure and actors

In drawing up the Organisation Structure, it is important to find out how stable it is and whether there are plans to reorganise when the new IT system is implemented. Where full organisational restructuring is required, the project team will need to include specialists with organisational and human factors skills.

Actors should be identified as required by the organisational structure. This will, to some extent, be influenced by the business activities they will be required to undertake. The definition of actors and their job specifications will be an iterative task.

Specify basic tasks

Terminology and notation vary widely; 'basic task' here is taken to mean a group of related business activities to be undertaken in response to one business event. This is different from the concept of 'task' which is taken to be the subset of business activities undertaken by a single actor/user role in response to a business event.

The Business Activity Model defines which business activities are triggered by each business event. The activities triggered by a business event are indicated by the line enclosing several activities in Figure 2-16.

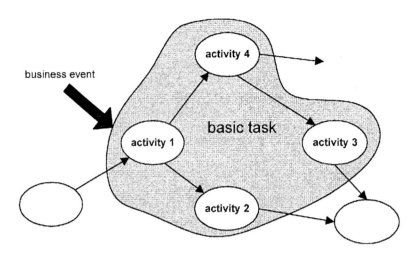

Figure 2-16 Business activities triggered by business event

The notation in Figure 2-16 is a general representation of part of a Business Activity Model. Ovals are activities and arrows between activities are dependencies.

Each dependency between activities within a basic task needs to be understood - does it represent provision of information, provision of some resource, or that one activity must be completed before another can start? An understanding of these dependencies will help to determine the optimum allocation of basic tasks to actors/user roles.

Specify interactions between tasks

Dependencies between activities in different basic tasks also have to be described; this applies both to different tasks for the same business event and tasks for different business events.

There may be multiple dependencies, and possibly complex interactions between tasks that can be carried out concurrently.

The application of techniques such as work flow analysis[2] attempt to reduce the number of interactions between tasks as this reduces the complexity of the overall business and leads to streamlining.

Allocate tasks to actors

Each basic task must be assigned to one or more actors. This volume does not prescribe a specific method for job design. It is strongly recommended that relevant expertise is used

---

[2] This approach to Business Process Re-engineering is described by a number of references, for example, *Business Process: Modelling and Analysis for Re-engineering and Improvement*, Martyn Ould, June 1995, Wiley.

in job design and that a job design method is adopted to be used in conjunction with Work Practice Modelling.

The subset of a basic task that is allocated to a single actor/user role is defined as a 'task'. Tasks defined in this way are used as the basis for Task Modelling. Note that it is likely that a single business event will require activities to be performed by more than one actor – in this case a single basic task will give rise to more than one task.

Co-operation between actors within business sub-systems should be defined. Also, co-operation between business sub-systems should be considered.

Specify interactions between actors and the IT system and identify user roles

In general, the Work Practice Model is concerned with the business system as a whole, which includes tasks that are completely manual as well as those which require some sort of interaction with the automated system. However, as an input to User Analysis, Task Modelling and subsequent specification and design activities within a project, it is necessary to focus attention on the needs of actors who will become users of the automated system.

There are three types of interaction between actors and the IT system:

- interaction with automated activities;

- obtaining IT support for manual activities;

- providing input to update the IT system.

Actors who have direct interaction with the IT system will be used as the basis for user roles.

Identifying user roles

User roles are the categories of actor who are given direct access to the IT system and will therefore become users of the IT system.

The aim of specifying user roles is to identify users who will require access to the same sets of functions and who can be given the same means of access to those functions. This is in order to avoid the situation where the same elements of dialogue are specified and designed twice just because they are required by two different groups of users.

There are several potential ways of identifying user roles:

- where different actors have been allocated to the same basic tasks they might be used to identify a single user role provided that their activities within the basic task are similar;

- User Analysis may highlight commonality between the requirements of different users;

- the authority structure within an organisation might equate to levels of access to the system that will be allowed. If a clerk and a supervisor share a number of common tasks but the supervisor will be allowed to view data to which the clerk will be denied access, these must be identified as separate user roles;

- external entities from the Required System Data Flow Model (see the *Function Modelling* volume in this series), if they are within the organisation, are often given names that will equate to user roles.

User roles are identified from the perspective of the intended usage of the automated system. In the simple case, it may only be necessary to identify a few user roles as the usage of the automated system will be the same whichever user is involved. Once user roles have been identified, they are used to determine the requirements for tasks which require access to the automated system and the supporting functions.

Allocate actors to job specifications

A job specification will combine sets of tasks undertaken by the same sets of actors. Job design skills are required to determine the optimum allocation of actors to jobs as the combination of skills possessed by the actors and the loading of individuals needs to be taken into account.

2.4.2 User analysis

This activity identifies who will use the system and what their user interface requirements are. It involves defining the different classes of user, listing the tasks they perform and describing the environment they work in. It produces the User Catalogue, User Class Descriptions and details of users' problems and requirements for inclusion in the Requirements Catalogue (see *The Business Context* volume in this series).

The aim of user analysis is to ensure that technical and end-user job design decisions are based upon an accurate appreciation of the user and job characteristics which might be affected by the proposed system.

An understanding of user skills and capabilities is important in user interface design. User analysis helps the development team to understand the benefits that are sought by future users of the automated system and the different types of presentation that may be required by different types of user. The capabilities and requirements of users needs to be understood to ensure that:

- design decisions are based on knowledge of users rather than the designers' assumptions;

- the user interface design satisfies the requirements of the full range of users of the system;

- users' motivations for using the new system are understood and taken into account;

- functionality included in the system is justified by user needs and business benefits.

User analysis is performed by collecting information about people and their jobs. The purpose of this is to gain a comprehensive view of users' jobs. Data of this kind can be collected by observation (more usefully 'commentary observation' where staff talk through what they are doing), questionnaires, discussions with personnel departments, workshops and by interviewing. If the introduction of the new automated system will be accompanied by a substantial change in job specifications, the analysis of jobs will need to be based upon what is proposed.

Areas of investigation may include the following:

- identification of elements of jobs undertaken by users;

- identification of goals of individuals and resolution of conflicts between goals;

- constraints on elements of jobs or activities undertaken by staff;

- interdependence/interaction with other staff;

- the existence of feedback on performance;

- sources of help when difficulties are encountered; interruptions/bottlenecks;

- variations in workload and strategies for coping with these variations;

- work organisation in different user locations if it is different;

- flexibility/autonomy for staff in organising their own work.

The activities of User Analysis are as follows:

- develop User Catalogue;

- determine user classes.

These are described in more detail in the following paragraphs.

Develop User Catalogue

The first activity of user analysis is to identify who the users of the new system will be. The emphasis is on future users, not users of current systems, unless they are the same.

The User Catalogue is simply a list of the members of the Organisation who will become users of the new system together with a description of the activities they perform.

The User Catalogue is developed by considering all the actors in the organisational structure and deciding whether the individuals concerned are likely to become users of the new IT system. This activity requires close consultation with key personnel. Although the User Catalogue is generally developed in the early stages of a project, the list of users (or potential users) may not be completely stable until the boundary of the new system has been selected.

Determine user classes

By understanding the capabilities and skills of the users, it should be possible to tailor the user interface to the needs of particular types of user to ensure optimum usability. Even where there is only one class of user it is useful to understand their skills and knowledge to ensure the usability of the new system.

By consideration of the users in the User Catalogue and using information available through interviews and observation, it should be possible to identify different classes of user. The classes should be distinct with as little overlap as possible.

Items that can be included are:

- **Level of IT sophistication**. This will depend on what the users are required to do in the current system and in the context of other computer-based systems such as the use of personal computers for word processing, electronic mail, e-commerce, etc.;

- **Users' expectations of the new system**. Some users will not believe that an automated system will be able to deliver what they require based on bad experiences of previous computer systems. Other users may desperately want a new system to help them in their work;

- **Degree of dedication**. It will be important to identify users who will be very regular users of the new system because the new system forms part of the business activities they perform. Other users may only need to use the system on an occasional basis. Some systems will have an uncontrolled population of users; for example, automatic telling machines or library systems. All of these factors will affect the style of the user interface, levels of help and the training required in the use of the new system;

- **Organisation culture/standards**. There may be organisational standards or practices with which user job specifications should conform; for example, how staff are expected to deal with others inside the organisation and with people from outside it - customers, the general public, the media, etc.;

- **Mandatory/discretionary use**. Some types of system require the users to use the system in order to perform their tasks, whereas other types of system are used as a by-product of the users tasks but the tasks are still basically performed manually;

- **Education/intellectual abilities**. Where the user population contains expertise in the use of computers and will be using the system in an 'expert' way there will be a need to reduce the amount of interaction with the system and to provide accelerating facilities such as short-cut keys. Where the user population is relatively unskilled, the interface must be much simpler and the amount of help increased. In reality any new system will probably have a mix of computer expertise;

- **Number of users in each user class**. A user class with a large population is likely to take precedence over a user class with only one member when deciding on the most appropriate mode of interaction with the system;

- **Training received/required**. If all users are familiar with a particular type of interface because of training received in the past, this should be taken into account

if a choice is to be made about the tools and technologies employed in the new
system;

- **Regular tasks**. It is useful to collect information on types of task that user classes
  will need to undertake most regularly.

The precise set of information collected and used will depend upon the organisational
environment and the type of system to be developed.

Representative users from each class should be observed and interviewed to help
determine the information required. It is important to talk to people who will actually use
the system wherever possible. Information can be collected using a wide range of
techniques such as observing users, questionnaires, facilitated workshops and
formal/informal interviews.

2.4.3 Task Modelling

Required Task Models are designed to meet the actors' and user roles' requirements for the
new business system which will incorporate the automated system. Required tasks are
initially identified from basic tasks as described above. Each task is undertaken by an actor
or user role in response to a business event.

Required Task Models can be developed independently of any knowledge of tasks
undertaken in the current environment. However, in the majority of cases, it will be
necessary to perform some sort of analysis of current tasks in order to ascertain some basic
parameters including the following:

- constraints in use that must be carried forward to the new system;

- problems with the current tasks that must be avoided;

- relative frequencies of tasks that can be used to assess likely frequencies of new
  tasks;

- information requirements and flows of information that may need to be supported in
  the new system;

- decisions that need to be made outside of any automated system that might
  influence the composition of tasks in the new system;

- levels of authority required to perform certain types of task.

The derivation of tasks is summarised in Figure 2-17.

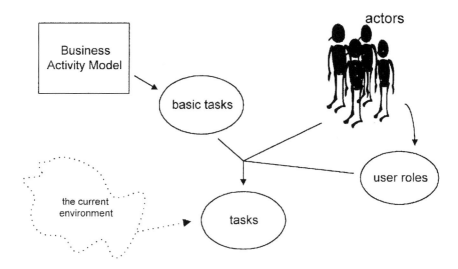

Figure 2-17 Derivation of tasks

The analysis of current tasks can be performed in a variety of different ways. Current Data Flow Models (see the *Function Modelling* volume in this series) will contain much of the information required. Alternatively, Current Task Models can be developed to give the analyst a clear definition of tasks undertaken in the existing organisation. The degree to which the current environment is studied and modelled will be directly influenced by the degree of change from the current business system to the required business system.

In Task Modelling, the analyst needs to consider the viewpoint of each user role and design appropriate task structures. These are developed by considering options for how tasks can be broken down and rationalised to reduce fragmentation of tasks and improve overall cohesion within the system. Within Task Modelling, the detailed allocation of elements of tasks between user and system will need to be explored.

Developing a Required Task Model

A task is that part of a basic task that is undertaken by a single actor or user role. A basic task is defined as the set of business activities triggered by a single business event. A Required Task Model is developed for each task. Therefore, the starting point for the development of a Required Task Model will be the list of Basic Tasks identified from the Business Activity Model.

The business activities in the Business Activity Model may have been decomposed to the level of sub-task. In this case, a number of business activities will be covered by a single Required Task Model. If it is considered appropriate, the Required Task Model can use the same basic notation as that used for the Business Activity Model – in this way Required Task Models can be seen as a development of the Business Activity Model rather than a completely new product. This will depend upon the method chosen for Business Activity Modelling and the tools used to construct the models.

The analyst should construct each Required Task Model from the set of business activities associated with a single task.

A hierarchy of sub-tasks is developed for each task below the level of detail in the Business Activity Model. Each task is then further described using a Task Description.

At the lowest level of decomposition, the sub-tasks will indicate task actions that will be performed by the actor/user role. These task actions will be either human only or human–computer actions which will be performed at the user interface. These task actions, taken from the complete set of Required Task Models, will form the basis of the user actions in the User Object Model and the information required to perform the complete set of tasks will form the basis of the definition of User Objects (see Chapter 3).

Develop Task Scenarios

A Task Scenario describes a situation that the user will recognise that works through a single task to a logical conclusion. Each Task Scenario is specific in that it does not deal in generalities; instead, it homes in on a particular set of circumstances and 'walks through' the task that needs to be performed in a thread which has a start point and a stop point.

Task Scenarios can be used to validate the Required Task Models but the development of a Task Scenario is likely to require additions or amendments to the Required Task Models. Thus Task Scenarios and Required Task Models are developed iteratively.

To develop a Task Scenario, the analyst writes down descriptions of examples of situations that users encounter. These help to ground the analysis in reality and allow all concerned to understand the detailed steps typical users go through and the information they need. The scenarios should be reviewed with users and used to refine the Required Task Models. Later, they can be used as the basis for the development of prototypes (see Chapter 6).

Getting the right Task Scenario mix and Task Scenario coverage

It is important when developing Task Scenarios to ensure that there is sufficient coverage of both normal and critical conditions as well as the more unusual and less important conditions. There is often a temptation to focus all scenarios on the interesting cases and ignore many frequent and common cases.

Scenarios should cover the following:

- common tasks and important business events;
- all users;
- critical but occasional events;
- some situations which are awkward to deal with;
- situations where people make mistakes;
- different working environments if this is an issue;

- current tasks and future (new) tasks;

- how any new technology will be used;

- some difficult and complex conditions;

- task boundaries and handovers;

- interleaving of tasks in likely sequences.

Scenarios should not:

- try to cover every condition;

- provide cases which users think are not worth considering;

- only cover correct usage of the system.

Scenarios should always be written from the user's perspective and look at their decision making.

In order to try to assess whether the set of Task Scenarios that have been developed have sufficient breadth and coverage, it is useful to develop a model which describes properties of the scenarios and compares them to the mix of circumstances found within the Organisation. Where there is a mismatch, this is likely to highlight the need for more scenarios to be developed. Also, this comparison will help the analyst to decide when enough scenarios have been written covering a particular area.

The Task Scenario coverage model is used to set targets and review the numbers of scenarios that are written in each area. It is developed after the first few scenarios have been written and when the important scenario properties are understood, based on an understanding of what is important to the users within the Organisation.

Inputs to the development of the coverage model include the following factors:

- an appreciation of major problems in the current system that need to be resolved in the new system;

- the User Catalogue (this is needed to determine how many users are within each user role);

- frequencies for different types of business events;

- a few example scenarios;

- an appreciation of the properties and coverage of each scenario.

Each Task Scenario has a number of aspects that can be assessed to evaluate its coverage. This can vary depending upon what is required. The three main aspects that are considered here are:

- how many users does this scenario involve?

- which organisational units are included in this scenario?

- how regularly are the tasks performed that are included in the scenario?

The example in Figure 2-18 shows how a number of scenarios are assessed under these three headings and percentages of scenario coverage compared to expected percentages in the set of Required Task Models.

User Population:	Booking Clerk	Supervisor	Telesales	Branch Mgr
Expected use	50%	20%	28%	2%
Scenario coverage	30%	18%	15%	5%
Evaluation of discrepancy	more scenarios required	reasonable match	may need more scenarios	no more scenarios required

Environment:	Front Office	Back Office	Maintenance
Expected use	50%	25%	25%
Scenario coverage	30%	23%	1%
Evaluation of discrepancy	more scenarios required	scenario coverage sufficient	more scenarios required

Frequent Tasks:	Walk-in Rentals	Allocation of Cars	Invoice Customers
Expected use	40%	23%	10%
Scenario coverage	90%	0%	0%
Evaluation of discrepancy	there are enough scenarios covering this area	some scenarios required here	some scenarios required here

Figure 2-18 Coverage of Task Scenarios

In the example here, the factors chosen to do the comparison are as follows:

- **User Population**. Is each section of the user population covered by at least one scenario? Are the user roles who will be expected to have the greatest involvement in the use of the system covered by the greater proportion of scenarios?

- **Environment**. Access will be given to the IT system in various different locations – do scenarios cover each of these different locations?

- **Frequent Tasks**. There are certain tasks which are key to the business and will be expected to be performed most regularly – do scenarios cover these frequent tasks more than the less frequent tasks?

In building the Task Scenario coverage model the focus should be on developing a minimum set of Task Scenarios that cover all the areas that are of importance to the users, and emphasis should be given to ensuring that coverage of these areas is in proportion to their occurrence within the business environment.

What level should scenarios be written at?

Task Scenarios should be written to show what it is anticipated to be like to work with the new system. They can be considered as the first prototype of the new system. Initially, they may be written to abstract out the details of how the system will work but later versions will be required with sufficient detail to drive a prototype.

Scenarios can also be written to summarise cases that the current system has to deal with as a way into understanding the current system if this is required.

2.4.4 Developing prototype designs

Early prototype designs will help to direct the analysis process and elicit relevant information. They will also help to validate the requirements as they have been understood so far. At this early stage it is useful to produce a small number of design alternatives to indicate the choices that are being considered. These designs can often be drawn on paper and talked through using one of the scenarios as a basis.

2.4.5 Specifying usability requirements

Critical usability requirements for the system are documented in the Requirements Catalogue, ensuring they are expressed in a form that can form the basis for testing. These requirements will be used to examine GUI design trade-offs and to identify priorities for the user interface design. Requirements can either refer to facilities or capabilities that the system must provide, or they can be expressed in terms of usability criteria.

The types of usability criteria that can be identified as part of Work Practice Modelling are as follows:

- productivity;
- learnability;
- user satisfaction;
- memorability;
- error rates.

These usability criteria are sometimes known as PLUME criteria.

An example of this type of requirement might be 'booking clerks having completed their training course should be able to complete a walk-in rental within five minutes with the new system with an error rate of less than one per hundred without reference to user manuals'. Another example might be 'managers should judge the system on average as 2 on a rating scale in which 1 signifies complete satisfaction and 7 complete dissatisfaction'.

2.4.6 Job design

Job design is an essential part of system development but when it is done from an IT perspective there is a danger that job design will be driven by the interface with technology – the user is left to do whatever is not done by the computer system. It is important that the actual effects of new systems on a person and their job are predicted and the jobs redesigned to the same degree as other parts of the system. A well-engineered job design will yield significant benefits for an organisation in terms of employee productivity and efficiency.

There is a large part of job design which is outside the scope of what most IT project practitioners would be expected to do within a project. There are three broad categories of job which need to be defined in relation to the automated system:

- jobs based on business activities which support the primary task. This type of job is very much rooted in the business and it would be a mistake to drive the specification of this type of job from the specification of how IT services are to be provided. It may be appropriate to bring in work practice experts to design these jobs;

- jobs based on servicing the information system (for example, data entry). This type of job is much more driven by the needs of the interface to the automated system;

- jobs based on primary task business activities which are to do with exploiting IT opportunities. In this case, IT practitioners and work practice specialists will need to work in co-operation.

Projects should choose a technique to define user jobs more formally as a part of the system development process. This technique should be driven by the users' roles and responsibilities rather than by the technological system solution.

Job design is based on the assembly of whole jobs in line with job design principles, user preferences (derived through user analysis) and Organisation policy and constraints. Job design criteria and usability requirements should be documented in the Requirements Catalogue.

2.5   Relationship with other analysis and design techniques

Below is a list of other analysis and design techniques with which Work Practice Modelling interfaces. A brief description is listed together with a reference to where the reader can find a full description of the technique.

2.5.1 Business Activity Modelling (covered in The Business Context volume)

The Work Practice Model is a mapping of the Business Activity Model onto an Organisation to specify:

- who (which user roles) carry out each business activity;

- where the activities are carried out.

The Business Activity Model includes business events which are used to identify basic tasks. These are used as the basis for tasks which are further defined in Required Task Models.

2.5.2 Data Flow Modelling (covered in Function Modelling volume)

The Current Physical Data Flow Model can be used as a source of information about current tasks that could be used as an input to Task Modelling.

2.5.3 Function Definition (covered in Chapter 4)

Functions can be derived from Required Task Models. Functions are the IT facilities which require to be controlled to provide direct support to tasks.

2.5.4 Requirements Definition (covered in The Business Context volume)

Some of the results of User Analysis are documented in the Requirements Catalogue as usability requirements. The development of the Work Practice Model, Required Task Models and Task Scenarios will generate functional requirements.

2.5.5 Prototyping (covered in Chapter 6)

Prototyping is an important tool in demonstrating the implications of the Required Task Models and Task Scenarios to users. Jobs which are designed to contain an element of on-line access should be prototyped to the users.

2.5.6 User Object Modelling (covered in Chapter 3)

The User Object Model is derived with direct reference to the Required Task Models.

2.5.7 User Interface Design (covered in Chapter 5)

All dialogues should be designed to support the user's job. User Interface Design should be user-centred rather than based upon the needs of the automated system.

3   USER OBJECT MODELLING

This chapter deals with the technique of User Object Modelling which is part of the overall construction of the user interface. The requirements for the user interface need to be specified at two levels:

- the user's mental model of the elements of the system (User Object Modelling);

- a representation of the interface in terms of windows and navigation through the system.

This chapter deals with the first of these points. The second is covered by User Interface Design (see Chapter 5).

Within the System Development Template, the User Object Model is an essential element of External Design in the area of Specification as shown in Figure 3-1.

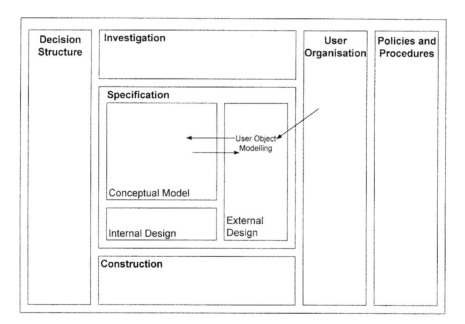

Figure 3-1 User Object Modelling in the System Development Template

The user interface is a vital part of the design of an automated system. For many systems, the user interface will be a complex area to design as it must fit in with the tasks of the user and be relatively straightforward to use. This requires techniques firstly to model the user interface and then to develop the interface design.

Overview

The User Object Model allows the analyst to identify, analyse and develop a model of what the user will think is 'in the system' and how it is structured and organised. The User Object Model identifies the information which should be presented at the user interface, what associations are important to users, and the rules and relationships that should be preserved at the user interface. The user objects are what the user believes he/she is seeing and interacting with in the user interface. It is needed to develop an effective organisation of the user interface which makes it easy for the users to learn and control the system.

The relationships between the User Object Model and other project products is shown in Figure 3-2.

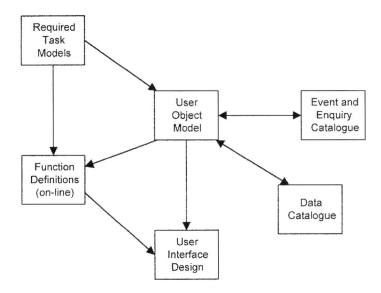

Figure 3-2 Relationship between the User Object Model and other analysis and design products

User Object Modelling is an important activity in the development of user interfaces because it determines how a potentially very confusing interface will be perceived by users, and hence how the system will be used. It pulls together the results of User Analysis and Task Modelling (see Chapter 2) to provide an overall framework for the design of the user interface. By developing the User Object Model in parallel with Entity Behaviour Modelling (see the *Behaviour and Process Modelling* volume in this series), the relationships and potential conflicts between the external view of the system and the logical internal view can be examined and contained.

The value of performing User Object Modelling is that it:

- focuses the designers' attention on how users will understand and hence use the system;

- supports the designer in achieving an appropriate match between the system and user tasks;

- provides a clear structured description of the system and its user interface;

- provides a framework for detailed design;

- forms a stable baseline against which design alternatives can be assessed.

The content of the user interface is derived from the User Object Model. What the user sees in windows is views of user objects upon which they will want to perform actions. The combination of windows and the constraints to be applied are dictated by the functions which in turn are based upon the definition of the users' tasks in the Required Task Models. The relationship between tasks, functions and the User Object Model is represented in Figure 3-3. For a full description of functions, see Chapter 4.

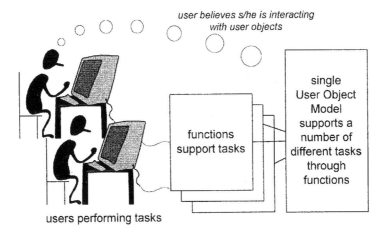

Figure 3-3 User Object Model, tasks and functions

Specification and design of the user interface do not need to be structured around the underlying processing requirements for the system because:

- the structure and content of the user interface is determined by the needs of the users;

- the structure and content of the underlying data and processing are determined by the requirements of the business and the needs of the system independent of the user organisation.

The 'system' view is represented by the events and enquiries interacting with the Logical Data Model while the 'user' view is represented by actions on the user objects defined in the User Object Model. These two views need to be co-ordinated at two levels:

- the subset of the User Object Model (UOM) attributes which represents structured persistent data should be represented by attributes and relationships in the Logical Data Model;

- events and enquiries in the Conceptual Model should be invoked by one or more user object actions (although not all actions will invoke events and enquiries).

This is represented in Figure 3-4.

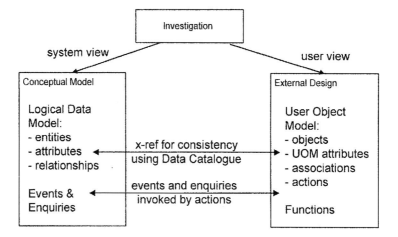

Figure 3-4 Relationship between user view of processing and system view

3.1 Concepts of User Object Modelling

In order to construct the User Object Model it is important to understand some of the basic concepts. These are described briefly here and described in more detail later in the chapter.

3.1.1 Actions

An action is something the user performs in relation to the user interface of the computer system. Actions can appear in three contexts:

- as elements of sub-tasks in Task Models (see Work Practice Modelling, Chapter 2);

- as properties of user objects – an action is a definition of what can be done by a user to interact with a user object;

- as part of GUI Design, where an action can be performed on controls within windows in the user interface. Window actions effectively implement user object actions. They are not one-to-one as several window actions may be required to implement one user object action and several user object actions could be implemented as a single window action.

The latter two types of action are described in this chapter.

It is through actions that the events and enquiries are invoked. All events and enquiries that are user initiated will be cross-referenced to actions. Not all actions will be cross-referenced to events and enquiries, however, as some act only within the context of the user interface without any effect on the stored data (modelled in the Conceptual Model).

3.1.2 Associations

An association is a relationship between two user objects that the system will need to provide or enforce. For example, if an action in one user object has a knock-on effect to a related user object or where there will be a requirement to navigate from one user object to another to complete a task. This can be demonstrated by the following case – if there is a user object 'Availability List' and another 'Car' an association is needed to navigate from the availability list to a specific car.

3.1.3 User objects

A user object is something the user will want to recognise as a component of the user interface of the automated system. A user object may represent one of three things:

- a set of data that the user wishes to view and/or change - this type of user object is likely to be related to elements of the Logical Data Model;

- a computer system user object or device with which the user will need to interact, for example, a printer;

- a container of other user objects or data, for example, a folder or directory. The container user object is usually uninteresting in its own right but it is useful for users to be able to move other user object types into and out of. This type of user object has the same notation as any other.

User objects are related to one another via associations, they have UOM attributes and they have actions associated with them.

3.1.4 UOM attributes

A UOM attribute is an element of a user object as defined by the user within the context of their tasks. UOM attributes are described in the Data Catalogue.

A proportion of UOM attributes will not have any equivalents in the Logical Data Model as they represent elements that are in the External Design but not in the Conceptual Model. However, where a UOM attribute is related to one or more Logical Data Model attributes, this is recorded in the Data Catalogue in the following way:

- in some cases, a UOM attribute will represent more than one attribute; for example, the user may consider Customer Name and Address to be a single UOM attribute whereas the Logical Data Model records Customer Name as a separate attribute from Customer Address. In this case, Customer Name and Address is recorded in the Data Catalogue as a data item that appears as a UOM attribute and it is cross-referenced to the data items Customer Name and Customer Address which appear as Logical Data Model attributes;

- in other cases, a UOM attribute will be directly equivalent to a Logical Data Model attribute; for example, Vehicle Registration Number in the User Object Model is equivalent to Registration Number which is an attribute of the Car entity in the Logical Data Model. The same entry in the Data Catalogue should be used to describe Vehicle Registration No and Registration Number. The data item could be called by either name and given a synonym to indicate the name used in the other model.

In this way, any cross-references between the Logical Data Model and User Object Model can be properly controlled and be sourced from a single set of definitions.

3.1.5 User Object Model

A User Object Model is, in essence, a user's mental model of the structure and contents of the system. It identifies simple mapping rules that will allow the user to predict how the system operates. It can be likened to the mental models we all hold of everyday things such as how to operate lights within a building. Whatever building we enter, we know where we expect to find light switches (just inside doors) and what will happen when we turn them on and off. As users of the light switches, we know that there must be an electrical connection between the light switches and the lights but it is not necessary to know about this in order to use them. User Object Modelling extends this concept to computer systems development and attempts to model the way in which the user would expect to navigate around the user objects within an automated system. A coherent and appropriate User Object Model means that the users will find things where they expect them to be and that they will behave in the way users expect them to behave. This is vital for the usability of any GUI-based interface.

It would be usual to build a single User Object Model for each application. However, if the key user objects of one group of user roles are almost entirely different from those of another, it may be appropriate to produce more than one User Object Model. Note that having two different User Object Models does not imply two different Conceptual Models – the different User Object Models could provide two different sets of users with access to the same underlying data and processing. An example from EU-Rent where two different User Object Models might be appropriate would be that users in the EU-Rent offices have a requirement to see different data from those users in the Maintenance Depots. The Car user object would be common to both models but different UOM attributes and actions would be appropriate to the two different sets of users.

3.2   Products of User Object Modelling

The product of User Object Modelling is the User Object Model. There would normally be one User Object Model for each application developed but there may be more than one where the user interface can be divided into distinct areas.

The User Object Model consists of the following products (see Figure 3-5):

- **User Object Structure**. This is a graphical representation of all user objects and how they relate together;

- **User Object Descriptions**. This is a description of the user objects including actions and UOM attributes for each user object.

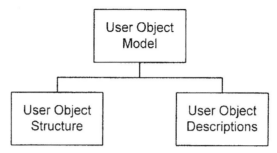

Figure 3-5 Structure for the User Object Model

These products are described in more detail in the following paragraphs.

3.2.1 *User Object Structure*

A User Object Structure is a pictorial representation of the user objects, together with their UOM attributes, actions and interrelationships.

The basic notation of a User Object Structure is shown in Figure 3-6.

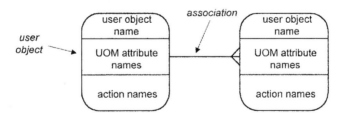

Figure 3-6 Structure conventions for User Object Structures

User Objects are represented by the boxes on the diagram which are 'soft boxes'. Each box represents a user object and consists of three areas:

- the user object name, put in the top part of the box;

- the UOM attribute names, listed in the central part of the box;

- the actions, listed in the bottom part of the box.

A user object contains the un-normalised information groupings that the user associates with the particular user object and the actions that they can perform on the whole user object or on some part of it.

An **association** is represented diagrammatically by a line that joins two user object boxes together. The conventions for associations are as follows:

- all lines are solid – there is no notation to indicate optionality. An association either exists or it does not;

- a crows foot indicates that each occurrence of the user object at the other end of the association can be associated with one or more occurrences of the user object at the end with the crows foot;

- the absence of a crows foot indicates that each occurrence of the user object at the other end of the association can be associated with only one occurrence of the user object at the plain end.

Using crows feet, it is possible to indicate one-to-one, one-to-many or many-to-many associations between user objects as shown in Figure 3-7.

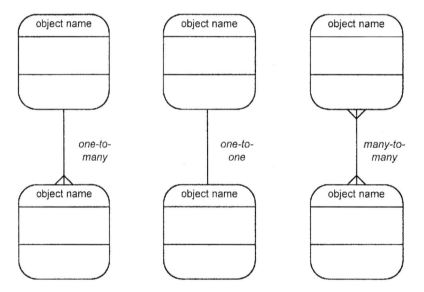

Figure 3-7 Cardinality of associations

The full notation for user objects may be considered too detailed for clarity for most diagrams. Therefore, a 'collapsed' version of the notation can be used for user objects as shown in Figure 3-8.

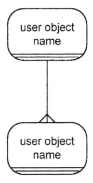

Figure 3-8 'Collapsed' notation for User Object Structure

The lines in the boxes denote these boxes as user objects without listing the UOM attributes or actions.

An example of a User Object Structure with the full notation taken from the EU-Rent example is shown in Figure 3-9.

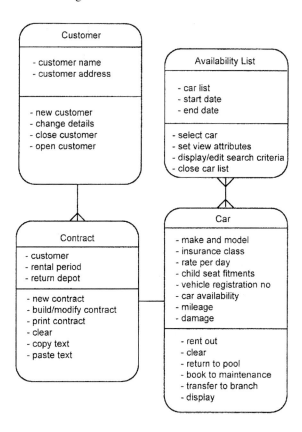

Figure 3-9 Example User Object Structure

This example is an initial view obtained from examining the task of handling a walk-in rental. The Availability List displays details of all cars available or only those cars which correspond to a set of criteria as specified by the customer. Details of any car on a list may be looked at to answer any queries the customer may have. When the customer accepts a car, the check-in clerk creates the contract which is printed and given to the customer. Note that the Car user object does not have any actions which correspond to creating or deleting instances of the car from the system – it is assumed that this is dealt with by the purchasing section who have their own User Object Model.

The full User Object Structure for the booking office area of EU-Rent using the 'collapsed' notation for user objects is shown in Figure 3-10.

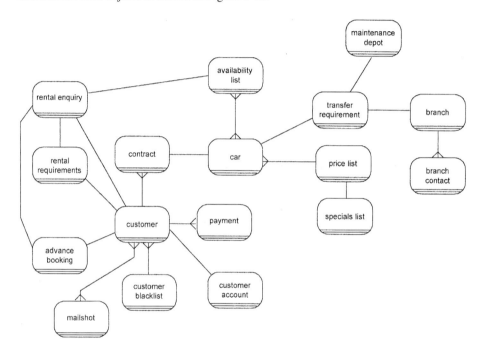

Figure 3-10 User Object Structure for EU-Rent

Note that this User Object Structure supports all the tasks of the branch staff including booking clerks and the branch manager. Different User Object Models would be developed for the maintenance depot staff and the purchasing section.

As an addition to the basic notation, a diamond notation can be used to indicate that user objects can be composed of other user objects as shown in Figure 3-11.

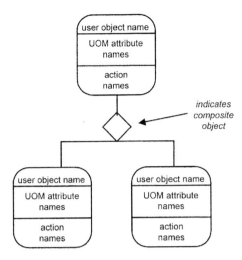

Figure 3-11 Nested user objects

Where user objects are shown connected by a diamond, the following applies:

- the user object above the diamond is the sum of the user objects below the diamond;

- the user objects below the diamond co-exist, they are not alternatives for one another;

- multiple occurrences of user objects are denoted in the same way as single occurrences; for example, a user object of Order could be composed of Order Header and Order Lines user objects.

3.2.2 User Object Description

For each user object in the User Object Structure there is an associated User Object Description. The contents of the User Object Description are:

- user object ID;

- user object name;

- user object text to describe the user object;

- for each action in the user object, a brief description of the resulting processing and/or change of state together with cross-references to UOM attributes and events/enquiries invoked by the action;

- a list of UOM attributes (completed where collapsed notation used).

An example User Object Description is shown in Figure 3-12.

User object: Car			
Description: Details of a car owned by EU-Rent which is available for rental			
Action	**Action Description**	**UOM Attributes**	**Events/Enquiries**
Rent out	Marks car as unavailable for renting	car availability	car allocation to rental walk-in rental
Clear	Removes car from user interface	–	–
Book to Maintenance	Marks car as unavailable for renting	car availability	service booking
Return to Pool	Marks car as available for renting, updates mileage and records damage	car availability mileage damage	return from service rental return car transfer
Transfer to Branch	Marks car as unavailable for renting	car availability	car transfer
Display	Displays all car details to user	all	car enquiry
UOM Attributes			
make and model, insurance class, rate per day, child seat fittings, mileage, damage, car availability			

Figure 3-12 Example User Object Description

All UOM attributes are documented in the Data Catalogue (see the *Data Modelling* volume in this series).

As mentioned before, a proportion of UOM attributes will not have any equivalents in the Logical Data Model as they represent elements that are in the External Design but not in the Conceptual Model. However, where a UOM attribute is related to one or more Logical Data Model attributes, this is recorded in the Data Catalogue.

In this way, any cross-references between the Logical Data Model and User Object Model can be properly controlled and be sourced from a single set of definitions.

3.3   The User Object Modelling Technique

The User Object Model allows the analyst to identify, analyse and develop a model of what the user will think is 'in the system' and how it is structured and organised. The user objects are what the user believes he/she is seeing and interacting with in the user interface. The actions are what the user expects to be able to do with the user objects and the associations are the connections that the user expects to find between user objects.

The User Object Model is usually developed after the Required Task Models have been completed and a number of Task Scenarios constructed to validate the Required Task

Models. The information required to perform tasks can be used to identify user objects and the lowest level sub-tasks can be used to identify actions on those user objects. The associations between objects are derived from the usage of the user objects by tasks – in many cases associations will represent navigation between user objects required to support tasks. All of this will need to be discussed in detail with the users to ensure that the User Object Model truly represents their mental model of the system.

The activities of User Object Modelling are expected to follow the progression shown in Figure 3-13. These activities are described in more detail in the following paragraphs.

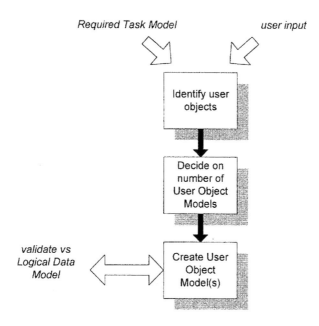

Figure 3-13 Tasks of User Object Modelling

3.3.1 Identify user objects

The aim of this activity is to identify the things (user objects) within the new system that users will need to monitor, control, transfer or modify through the user interface. All types of user object identified in this way will appear in some form as user objects in the User Object Model.

The two main inputs to the identification of user objects are as follows:

- **Required Task Model**. In identifying the required tasks of the system, the user objects required by the tasks should also have been identified. These may be documented within the Task Descriptions (see Chapter 2);

- **Interviews with users**. By talking through the user interface with users, user objects may be identified as being required in the user interface. The type of user object identified in this way is likely to be a general-purpose type of user object that the user does not consider to be specific to tasks.

When attempting to identify user objects, it is worth bearing in mind that some user objects are likely to correspond with entities or groups of entities in the Required System Logical Data Structure whereas others will not have any equivalents in the Logical Data Model as they are features of the user interface alone. In general, user objects that appear in the User Object Model differ from entities in the Logical Data Model in several ways:

- some user objects are not entities at all; for example, artefacts such as documents or printers or mailboxes that would not be stored in the database at all, or collections of information, such as diaries or catalogues, which may be derived from multiple entity occurrences;

- many of the user objects are composites of the entities on the Logical Data Model which are not even approximately normalised. For instance, the whole of an accident report form in EU-Rent could be one user object;

- many-to-many and one-to-one associations between user objects are common;

- some entities or groups of entities will appear in more than one user object. For instance, an EU-Rent user would almost certainly think of an application for a corporate account being different from customer details. This would be because the user knows that different actions are associated with applications and customers so they would be different user objects in their mental model. On the other hand, in data modelling terms, the application holds potential customer information and would therefore probably be considered as a customer with a different status from existing customers. The two user objects would be modelled as a single entity (or group of entities) within the Logical Data Model.

The names of user objects, UOM attributes and actions should reflect terms used in the day-to-day business. The names should reflect concepts that the user readily understands, not the analyst's interpretation of those terms.

Part of the Required Task Model for the task Walk-in Rentals is shown in Figure 3-14. This is the part of the model which involves the user in trying to identify a suitable car for the rental request based upon the requirements expressed by the customer.

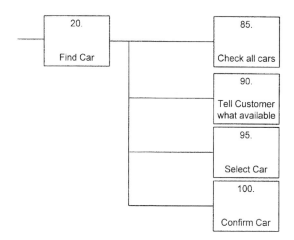

Figure 3-14 Part of Required Task Model for Walk-in Rental

By examining the information required to support this part of the task, we can identify the following user objects:

- **Rental Requirement** – the user will need to record details of the requirements of the customer for a car in order for the system to identify suitable cars;

- **Availability List** – the user will need to look at a summary of all cars that are available before identifying a particular car for this rental;

- **Car** – it will be necessary for the user to view details of the car before offering it to the customer.

This is a starting point for the User Object Model. It is built up and modified by looking at all the tasks that are performed on this type of information. By building a generalised model of the user objects, this will ensure that the user will be presented with a consistent interface which will have similar behaviour in a number of different contexts. For example, the user would expect the availability list to be used to support a number of different tasks, for example, dealing with telephone enquiries as well as walk-in rentals, and would expect it to behave in a similar way each time it is used.

At the point of identifying user objects, it might be useful to do a quick comparison with the Required System Logical Data Model to check that the set of user objects is compatible with the entities. If data represented by user objects is persistent it should be present in the Logical Data Model. If data has been included in the Logical Data Model it should be clear how the user will access it via user objects.

3.3.2 *Decide on number of User Object Models*

There is a choice between developing a single User Object Model for all user roles or producing one User Object Model for each user role or group of user roles.

To help in this decision, it is helpful to identify first those user objects that are central to the tasks of the user roles – the key user objects. These key user objects should be analysed to identify those whose UOM attributes are equivalent to the attributes defined in the Required System Logical Data Model. Such user objects will possibly be parts of entities in the Required System Logical Data Model and others will possibly span more than one entity. This will help to identify user objects with common or similar data.

There are several circumstances in which it is preferable to produce more than one User Object Model:

- if the key user objects of one user role are almost entirely different from those of another user role, it may be appropriate to produce a different User Object Model for each user role (in fact, this may also help in deciding on partitioning of the system for development);

- if user roles share the same user objects but will be interested in different UOM attributes of the user objects and/or will want to perform distinctly different actions on them.

The production of separate User Object Models will cut down the complexity in each model. However, if a user object appears in more than one model, it is important to ensure that the user object has similar core UOM attributes and behaviour in both models, even if there are minor variations. This will help to maintain consistency in the user interface for users that can adopt more than one user role.

Wherever user objects are common between two or more user roles it is probably better to produce a composite User Object Model. This will allow an end-user to move from one role to another without having to change their mental model of the common area.

3.3.3 Create User Object Model(s)

The first task above identified all user objects. The second task identified the need for one or multiple User Object Models. The next task is to build the User Object Model(s), connecting the user objects with the appropriate associations. Also, at this point the user objects are fully defined and cross-referenced to the Required System Logical Data Model.

To analyse the associations between user objects it is useful to work from the point of view of a single user object and consider the other types of user object to which it is directly related. This can be done in the following ways:

- the Required System Logical Data Model can be used as an input to this task. Some of the associations between user objects will mirror relationships on the Required System Logical Data Model or will be associated because of sharing common data;

- the Required Task Models will define the usage of user objects and will suggest associations between them.

Once an association has been identified between two user objects, it is necessary to define its cardinality (one-to-many, many-to-many or one-to- one). Again, the Required Task

Models and Required System Logical Data Model may help in this as may consultation with the users.

The associations identified above will help the analyst construct the basic User Object Structure. To complete the User Object Model, it is necessary to define the UOM attributes and actions for each user object, either written into the user objects on the diagram or documented using User Object Descriptions.

All of the UOM attributes should be documented as data items in the Data Catalogue. Where a UOM attribute represents multiple attributes from the Logical Data Model, these should be cross-referenced in the Data Catalogue. Where the UOM attribute is equivalent to an attribute from the Logical Data Model, these should be described by the same entry in the Data Catalogue and cross-referenced to both models. In some cases, the addition of a UOM attribute may prompt the creation of an extra attribute in the Logical Data Model. By looking at the attributes in the Logical Data Model this may help to identify the need for UOM attributes in the User Object Model. This will help to ensure consistency between the two models throughout.

Some UOM attributes may be added later, as the interface develops during prototyping.

The actions for a user object can be identified from the relevant Required Task Models. These will be actions to be performed on the user objects, such as Print, Select or Authorise. Most user objects will have actions for creation and deletion. An exception to this might be where there is more than one User Object Model for an application, each containing different views of the same user object; for example, in the EU-Rent application the user object Car would appear in the User Object Model for the branch rental staff and also in the User Object Model for the purchasing section. The purchasing section would be responsible for creating and removing cars – the branch rental staff would only deal with the movements of the cars.

Further actions may be added during prototyping and evaluation (see Chapter 6).

3.4   Relationship with other analysis and design techniques

Below is a list of other analysis and design techniques with which User Object Modelling interfaces. A brief description is listed together with a reference to where the reader can find a full description of the technique.

3.4.1 *Work Practice Modelling (covered in Chapter 2)*

The User Object Model is derived initially with reference to the information required to support tasks performed by all user roles. Where groups of user roles are interested in completely different sets of key objects, there may be a need to develop several User Object Models.

Actions and UOM attributes are also derived with reference to the required tasks. Associations will support the navigation requirements of the tasks.

3.4.2 Logical Data Modelling (covered in the Data Modelling volume)

The entities on the Logical Data Model can generally be cross-related to User Objects. In addition the UOM attributes are held in the Data Catalogue and can be cross-referenced (in both directions) to the attributes documented for the entities.

3.4.3 Function Definition (covered in Chapter 4)

Functions are the units of processing within the user interface which give direct support to tasks. Functions are cross-referenced to those areas of the User Object Model that are required for a particular task or sub-task.

3.4.4 User Interface Design (covered in Chapter 5)

The User Object Model is a primary input to User Interface Design. The user objects and their associations are supported by windows and window navigation. Window actions are an implementation of user object actions.

4   FUNCTION DEFINITION

Function Definition identifies units of processing specification, or functions, which need to be controlled as a whole in order to support the user's tasks.

During the development project two types of function are identified;

- **On-line functions**, where the user interfaces directly with the system either to update some of the information stored within the system or to retrieve information stored by the system or, more normally, a combination of the two.

- **Off-line functions**, where the system operates without user intervention (e.g., back-up). This type of function is sometimes known as a Batch function.

This volume deals solely with on-line functions. Off-line functions are described in the *Function Modelling* volume in this series.

Within the System Development Template, functions are the essential building blocks of External Design within Specification as shown in Figure 4-1.

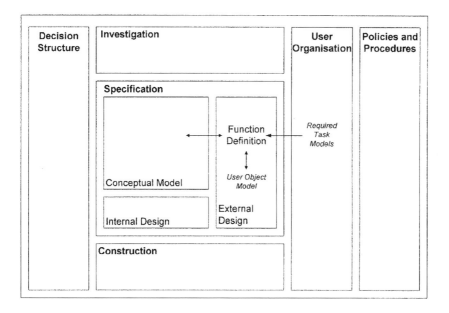

Figure 4-1 Function Definition in the System Development Template

Function Definition has several purposes:

- it identifies and defines the units of system processing required to support user tasks. These will then be carried forward to physical design where they will be implemented;

- it pulls together the products of analysis and design, which together specify a function;

- it identifies how best to organise the system processing to support the user's tasks which have been defined in Work Practice Modelling;

- it develops and confirms a common understanding between the analyst and the user of how the system processing is to be organised;

- it provides a basis for sizing and for deriving design objectives.

4.1   Concepts of Function Definition

A function is a unit of processing which is required to be controlled as a whole in support of a single task. Where the task requires several units of processing which do not directly interact, and do not need to be controlled together, there will be more than one function defined for that task.

The relationship between tasks and functions is represented in Figure 4-2. The task includes all the activities the user needs to perform in response to a single business event - functions provide the automated parts of the task.

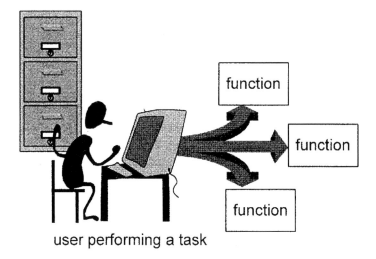

Figure 4-2 Tasks and functions

As described in the previous chapter (User Object Modelling), user objects represent features of the user interface with which the user interacts. Functions define which of the user objects are required for tasks and what subset of the total actions for that User Object are actually required to support the specific task. Therefore if a particular task requires access to, for example, two user objects and only four of the actions within each object, this will be defined in the functions supporting that task.

Many of the tasks defined will share common sub-tasks. Each common sub-task will be supported by a function or function component. This leads to the identification of common function components. These are individual functions, or parts of functions, which are shared by a number of different tasks. Separating these out, at this stage, will assist with defining processing components that can be re-used in a number of different functions.

This concept is represented in Figure 4-3.

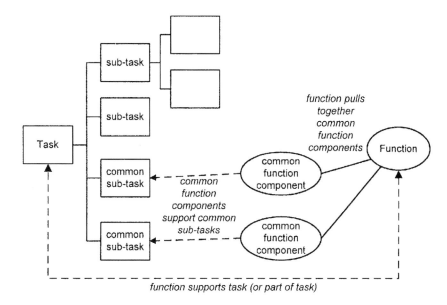

Figure 4-3 Tasks, common sub-tasks, functions and common function components

Functions can contain elements which are either on-line or off-line (batch). The function elements which are on-line require a user interface and are therefore defined in a different way from function elements which operate without a user interface.

There are three levels that need to be defined in order to be able to implement the processing required by an on-line function. These three levels are represented in Figure 4-4.

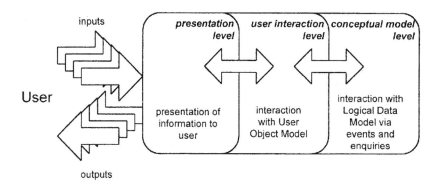

Figure 4-4 Levels within a function

The three levels within a function represent the following concepts:

- **the presentation level** is the presentation of the function to the user. The same presentation may be used for more than one function. In some systems, it is possible to switch views at this level without changing the core objects or actions available to the user. An example of this would be the switching between 'Normal' and 'Page Layout' views in a word processing package;

- **the user interaction level** is where the user executes actions on user objects. There will be a number of actions that only operate at this level and others that will progress to the next level (conceptual model level). Examples of actions that remain at this level would be zooming, printing or keying in information before a 'save' action invokes an event;

- **the conceptual model level** is where an action invoked in the interface level is recognised as invoking an event or enquiry that requires access to the underlying persistent data as represented in the Logical Data Model. The action is interpreted into the appropriate event or enquiry trigger which is applied to the Logical Data Model in the way specified in Entity Behaviour Modelling (see the *Behaviour and Process Modelling* volume in this series). This level is specified by the cross-references between the User Object Model and events and enquiries.

4.2   Products of Function Definition

The product of the Function Definition technique is the Function Definition.

All functions are documented by a largely textual document called the Function Description. This describes the important features of the function and details cross-references to related products. The precise composition of the Function Description will be different depending upon whether the function is fully on-line, fully off-line or a mixture of both.

For on-line elements of functions, which are relatively complex there may be a need to develop a Function Navigation Model. This will be used as the basis for the Window Navigation Model developed during User Interface Design.

The Product Breakdown for a Function Definition is shown in Figure 3-5.

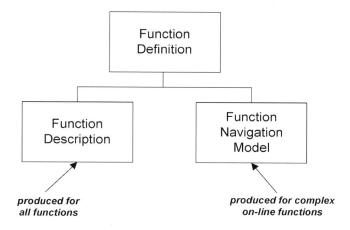

Figure 4-5 Product Breakdown Structure for Function Definition

4.2.1 Function Description

A Function Description contains some descriptive text and a large number of cross-references to other products. The precise format of the product will depend upon the documentation tools available to the project. An example of a typical Function Description for an on-line function is given in Figure 4-6. A subset of this will be completed for a common function component.

Function ID and Name: F1 – Walk-in Rental	
Function Type	Implementation Type: On-line Process Type: Update Initiation Type: User Initiated
Task x-ref	1: Walk-in Rental
User Roles x-ref	Booking Clerk
Common function component x-ref	10: Define Requirements for Rental 15: Check Customer 20: Find Car 25: Accept Payment
Function Text	This function supports the task 'Walk-in Rental'. It co-ordinates a number of common function components which together allow the user to complete a contract for the rental. The function allows the user to enter all the details relevant to the Walk-in Rental and when the details are confirmed, the function then prints out the contract for the customer to check and sign and confirms the allocation of the selected car to the rental. The user can amend details relating to customer requirements and can select another car if the customer is not satisfied with the contract. The function is closed after the final contract is printed and the user confirms OK.

The common function components are controlled as follows (see related Function Navigation Model).

10: Define Requirements for Rental	This is either initiated directly by the user or from 20:Find Car. The date and time of the rental should default to today's date and time. The branch for pick-up should default to this branch. Results of this function component are used to drive the availability list in 20:Find Car.
15: Check Customer	This is initiated directly but it must be completed before 20:Find Car can be initiated.
20: Find Car	This can either be initiated automatically from 10:Define Requirements for Rental or via user intervention after 15:Check Customer is completed. Search criteria can either look for all available cars if no requirements have been set, defaulting to today's date and time, or use Car Group from 10:Define Requirements. In this case, use any other requirements specified as secondary criteria on search.
25: Accept Payment	Calculate payment based on car selected plus options.

Potential Problems	For walk-in rental, if no suitable car found, should ring nearest EU-Rent branch and attempt to locate suitable car. If not, refer to company policy re substitutions. If no suitable match found, suggest alternative companies in the area.

User Object Model References	**User Object Name**	**Actions**
	Contract	All
	All objects and actions used by common function components	
Requirements Catalogue entries x-ref	0034: Provide support for walk-in rentals	
Related functions	N/A	
Volumes	See Task frequency – function will be once per task. Usage of common function components: 15: 1 per function 10: 1.5 per function 20: 1.5 per function 25: 0.8 per function	
Windows/ dialogues x-ref	Not yet defined	
Service Level Requirements	The function must be fast enough to support discussion between branch staff and the customer such that the total task can be completed in 5 minutes. Availability: between 8 a.m. and 6 p.m., Monday through Saturday.	

Figure 4-6 Example Function Description

The properties of a function that are recorded on a Function Description for an on-line function/common function component are as follows:

- **Function ID**. A unique identifier;

- **Function name**. A name that describes the processing contained in the function;

- **Function Type**. There are three ways of classifying functions. Each function should have an entry for all three classifications;

    i.   **Implementation Type** – in this case it is always 'on-line' (for off-line functions it would be 'off-line'):

    ii. **Process Type** – either update or enquiry (U or E);

    iii. **Initiation Type** – either user or system (U or S) - where the initiation type is 'system' the function would usually be 'off-line'.

- **Cross-reference to task or sub-task**. If the function is one-to-one with a task, this is a reference to that task. If the function covers only one sub-task within a task, or a common sub-task, this reference is put here;

- **Cross-reference to user roles**. The user roles of the tasks that can use the function or common function component;

- **Function Text**. A brief description of the function including what causes the function to be invoked, what the system does in response to that input and the output produced by the function. It should include any requirements from the user about how the function is to be presented as this will be helpful in User Interface Design. Where common function components are to be included in this function, a description of any controls to be applied to each of the function components is included here;

- **Potential problems**. An overview of any exceptions that may be encountered during the execution of the function. This should be used as an informal way of noting down information as it is discovered. Some of the validation checks will be defined in the Data Catalogue. Any that are specific to the function processing at the user interface can be described in outline here. Basic syntax validation should not generally be included;

- **Cross-reference to User Object Model**. The function will require access to user objects and certain actions on those user objects will be required to support the function. This should not include all possible actions that the user can use as general facilities across all functions – it should only cover those actions that are needed to execute the function;

- **Cross-reference to Requirements Catalogue Entries**. The Requirements Catalogue Entries related to the function;

- **Related functions**. A reference to any related function. An example is where an off-line function stores errors on a transient data store. The errors are later corrected on-line. Two functions would be created but cross-referenced to each other;

- **Volumes** (frequency of use of function). A clear indication should be given of the number of occurrences of the function being used in a given time period – this will be based on the frequency of tasks. If there are any significant peaks or troughs anticipated, in any time cycle, these should be noted. For example, the same function could undergo seasonal fluctuations through the year, more local fluctuations on a monthly basis and have peaks and troughs through the working day. This volumetric information will be needed to assess the viability of the Service Level Requirements and to predict the capacity requirements during Technical System Options;

- **Cross-reference to windows and dialogues**. The windows and dialogues designed as part of User Interface Design which are used to access the function;

- **Service Level Requirements**. These consist of the following:

    - **Description** (textual description of the service level requirement);

    - **Target Value** (quantitative expression of performance, size, cost satisfaction levels, etc.);

    - **Range** (maximum and minimum target value);

    - **Comments** (any comment which qualifies the target value and acceptable ranges).

4.2.2 Function Navigation Model

For very complex functions it may be useful to construct a diagram which shows how the different parts of the function relate to each other. This can be done either informally by walking through the different parts of the function or formally by the construction of a Function Navigation Model.

This model can be used:

- to aid the analyst in understanding the function;

- to help validate the function with the users;

- as an input to the construction of the Window Navigation Model (see Chapter 5).

It is expected that this model will not be produced for most functions, rather being only produced for very complex ones.

The Function Navigation Model shows navigation between function components and the main function processing. The basic notation for a Function Navigation Model is shown in Figure 4-7.

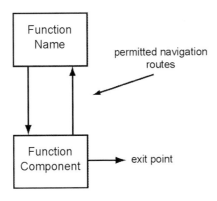

Figure 4-7 Basic notation for Function Navigation Model

A structure is built up where the boxes represent either main function or the a common function component. The arrows between the boxes represent permitted navigation paths for this function.

An example Function Navigation Model from the EU-Rent system for the Walk-in Rental function is shown in Figure 4-8.

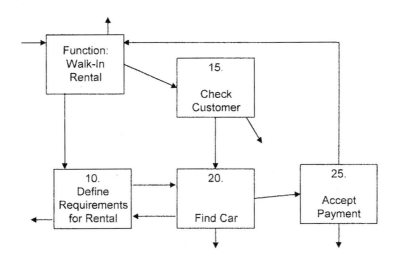

Figure 4-8 Example Function Navigation Model for Walk-in Rental

In this example the top left box, Walk-in Rental, represents the main function and all the other boxes represent common function components. At first the analyst decided that the Issuing of the Contract should be separated out as a common function component. However, after validation of this with the user it has been decided, for security reasons, that the issuing of the contract should not be defined as a common function component and therefore its processing is contained within the main function box. Arrows between boxes show permitted navigation. Arrows not to a box show exit points from the function.

4.3 The Function Definition Technique

Function Definition consists of a number of activities which are as follows:

- identify functions;

- specify functions;

- validate and complete functions.

These activities are described in more detail in the following paragraphs. The following diagram shows the relationship between functions and other development products. This can be used as an aid to reading the technique.

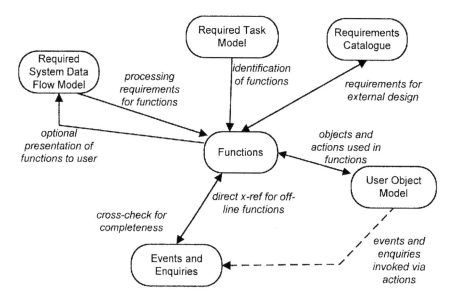

Figure 4-9 Relationship between functions and other products

4.3.1 Identify functions

The main input to the identification of functions is the set of Required Task Models. Each task that requires support from the automated system will require one or more functions.

Each common sub-task that requires automated support will provide one or more common function components. Where the common sub-task is used within tasks, the common function components will also be used.

If a particular common function component can operate independently of the rest of the functionality of the task, it will become a function in its own right. Where a common function component needs to be controlled or co-ordinated with other areas of functionality to support the task, it will be incorporated into a function.

For each task, the following activities will help to identify functions:

- determine whether the task requires automated support. If it does, there will be at least one function identified;

- decide whether the complete set of functionality for a task needs to be controlled or coordinated as a unit – in this case there will be a one single function for a task. Where there are areas of functionality which do not require to be controlled as a unit (for example, stand-alone enquiries which are optional), these may be identified as a number of separate functions;

- by looking at the task, determine whether there are any common sub-tasks incorporated within the task. Each common sub-task leads to the identification of one or more common function components. Decide whether these common function components can operate independently of the functions supporting the task, in which case they become functions in their own right. Where the common function components needs to be coordinated within another function or with other common function components, decide the controls required to ensure the components fit together as they should do within the function;

- the functions identified from the Required Task Models will be 'user-initiated' functions as the tasks are constructed from the perspective of the actors/user roles within the business. Functions identified in this way will tend to be on-line functions. It is possible, however, for there to be parts of the function that, although the function is user initiated, are actually off-line function components.

In discussion with users and by considering users' tasks the requirement for enquiries within update functions should be considered. This does not include reads required to select entity occurrences in order to carry out the updating required for an event. They are enquiries to be done to provide the user with information either as a precursor or as a by-product of the events.

An example of an enquiry forming part of an update function from EU-Rent is where the user is recording details of cars that have been delivered. The update associated with the event Car Delivered must be preceded by an enquiry which informs the user whether this delivery is expected or not. The function will encompass both the enquiry and the update each identified as a separate function component.

It is important that users are involved in the identification of functions. Functions must support the tasks that the users are required to perform. The automated system will not exist in isolation.

4.3.2 Specify functions

As each function is identified it is documented using the Function Description.

The User Object Model contains user objects and actions that are required to support the user's tasks. The user objects and actions required by a particular function should be cross-referenced from the Function Description. There may be additional on-line functions identified by examination of the User Object Model.

The Required System Data Flow Diagrams can be used to add more detail about the underlying processing requirements of all types of function. The majority of functions described in the Required System Data Flow Model will be update functions but major enquiry functions may also be shown on the Required System Data Flow Diagrams. These can be used to cross-check the set identified using the technique above. This way of deriving functions is covered in the *Function Modelling* volume in this series.

The Required Task Models and Required System Data Flow Model are complementary products – the Required Task Models are analysing user tasks and the functions from the user's perspective whereas the Data Flow Model does not model the interaction with the user in detail but can specify some of the underlying processing and data accesses required to support functions.

When functions are first identified not all the information required to complete the Function Definition documentation will be available. As the information becomes available at different points in the method the Function Description should be progressively updated.

4.3.3 Validate and complete functions

As described above, functions are identified from the Required Task Models and a number of other possible sources. Functions are specified with reference to a number of other products. Once functions have been specified in this way, they can then be checked and updated:

- the User Object Model can be used to check functions by ensuring that all user objects and actions are used by at least one function. Any user objects and actions that are not used by functions should be examined carefully, possibly requiring new functions to be created;

- events and enquiries can be used to check functions by ensuring that all events and enquiries that require user interaction are used by at least one function;

- User Interface Design, together with Prototyping, can be used to check functions as new requirements may come to light when windows are designed and shown to the users.

Service level requirements may be recorded against functional requirements in the Requirements Catalogue. These are transferred to the Function Description where appropriate during Function Definition.

Volumetrics are important as an input to Capacity Planning and system sizing. Estimated frequencies of function usage should be documented as early as possible to allow sizing to be performed in Technical System Options and Physical Design.

Functions cannot be completed until User Interface Design has been completed as functions need to be cross-referenced to the products of User Interface Design.

4.4   Ad hoc enquiries

There may be a type of enquiry which cannot be pre-defined but which will be created by the user as and when required. This type of enquiry clearly cannot be defined as a normal function, but some assumptions need to be made about the type, complexity and frequency of such enquiries so that they are at least considered when system sizing and timing is carried out.

A Function Description should be developed for each user role that will be able to formulate this type of enquiry. The Function Text will be the only entry completed for these enquiries. It should contain the following details:

- entities likely to be accessed by the user role in the creation of ad hoc enquiries;

- means of enquiry (by screen or report);

- type of data manipulation to be allowed for the user role (read only, comparison or calculation).

The purpose of recording these details is to ascertain areas that will be of interest to the user role and to ensure that the impact of enquiries is at least considered during Physical Design.

4.5   Relationship with other techniques

Below is a list of other analysis and design techniques with which Function Definition interfaces. A brief description is listed together with a reference to where the reader can find a full description of the technique.

4.5.1 *Logical Data Modelling (covered in the* Data Modelling *volume)*

Enquiry functions or enquiry fragments of functions will validate that the Required System Logical Data Model can support the enquiry requirements. This may result in changes to the Logical Data Model being necessary.

4.5.2 Work Practice Modelling (covered in Chapter 2)

The tasks derived as part of Task Modelling will be used as the main input to the identification of on-line functions. Required Task Models are examined to identify whether a function is for the whole task or for sub-tasks requiring a user interface. Task Scenarios may help in the validation of functions.

4.5.3 Entity Behaviour Modelling (covered in Behaviour and Process Modelling volume)

All events and enquiries will be invoked via functions (this relationship is indirect where a User Object Model exists – in this case actions from the User Object Model invoke events and enquiries – functions then cross- reference the actions).

The identification of functions often identifies the need for events and enquiries. Conversely, the examination of events and enquiries may help to determine what functions are required.

As Event Identification and Entity Life History Analysis are carried out events will be identified. These events must be cross-referenced by functions. New functions may be created or existing functions amended.

4.5.4 User Interface Design (covered in Chapter 5)

Functions are cross-referenced to the user objects and their actions. This cross-reference will be used as an input to the identification of views required for User Interface Design. Function Navigation Models will be a major input to the Window Navigation Model.

4.5.5 Prototyping (covered in Chapter 6)

Prototyping may help to identify errors or inconsistencies in the Function Definition documentation. Any changes needed are fed back to Function Definition.

4.5.6 Requirements Definition (covered in The Business Context volume)

Requirements for enquiries are likely to be documented in the Requirements Catalogue. These enquiry requirements are developed into enquiries which are used by functions or components of functions.

Service level requirements may be recorded against functional requirements in the Requirements Catalogue. These are transferred to the Function Description where appropriate during Function Definition.

5   USER INTERFACE DESIGN

This chapter deals with the technique of User Interface Design. User Interface Design is used to capture the user's requirements for the user interface and represent the on-line activities of a system.

The User Interface Design is a representation of the interface in terms of windows and navigation through the system. The approach described here is of particular applicability to user interfaces which will be implemented using a Graphical User Interface (GUI) and also can be used to design interfaces that will be used on the internet.

Although User Interface Design is very much influenced by the actual tools and technologies used for the implementation of the interface, it is an area that can greatly influence the specification of the system at an early stage in the development lifecycle and is therefore addressed here rather than in the Physical Design.

Within the System Development Template, the User Interface Design is an essential element of External Design in the area of Specification as shown in Figure 5-1.

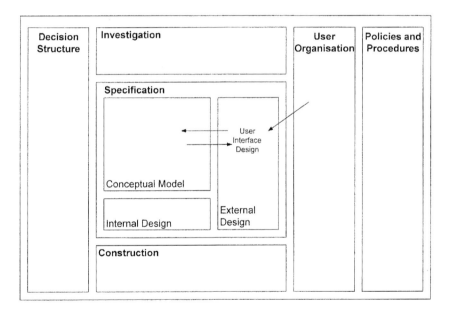

Figure 5-1 User Interface Design techniques in the System Development Template

The user interface is a vital part of the design of an automated system. For many systems, the user interface will be a complex area to design as it must fit in with the tasks of the user and be relatively straightforward to use.

This requires techniques firstly to model the user interface (see Chapter 3) and then to develop the interface design.

User Interface Design ensures that user roles from the User Organisation are given access to the elements of the stored data in a controlled and usable way. User Interface Design concentrates on the user's direct interaction with the system and is therefore of utmost importance in the analysis and design of a usable system.

Overview

The relationships between the User Interface Design and other development project products is shown in Figure 5-55.

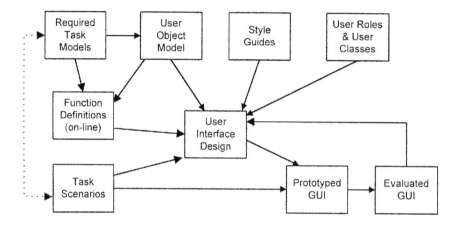

Figure 5-2 Relationship between User Interface Design products and other products

The User Interface Design is initially developed from six main products:

- Required Task Models;
- Task Scenarios;
- User Object Model;
- Function Definitions;
- Installation Style Guide;
- Application Style Guide.

The content of the user interface is derived from the User Object Model. What the user sees in windows is views of user objects upon which they will want to perform actions. The combination of windows and the constraints to be applied are dictated by the functions which in turn are based upon the definition of the users' tasks in the Required Task Models.

The Installation Style Guide and Application Style Guide form the mechanism used to ensure that the installation and application standards are applied to screen and report layouts.

An important part of designing a user interface is the feedback from prototyping and evaluation (see Chapter 6). The design of the user interface involves demonstrating early designs to users and having them evaluate the design. Although the two topics are described independently, User Interface Design and Prototyping and Evaluation are very much interrelated.

5.1 User Interface Design Concepts

This section describes the concepts of User Interface Design.

5.1.1 Action

An action is something the user performs in relation to the user interface of the computer system. Actions can appear in three contexts:

- as elements of sub-tasks in Task Models (see Chapter 2);

- as properties of user objects - an action is a definition of what can be done by a user to interact with a user object;

- as part of GUI Design where an action can be performed on controls within windows in the user interface. Window actions effectively implement user object actions. They are not one-to-one as several window actions may be required to implement one user object action and vice versa.

The latter two types of action are described in this chapter.

5.1.2 Window

A window is effectively a communication channel through which the user looks to view and interact with user objects from the User Object Model. Ideally, the context of the window should not affect the basic features and behaviour (UOM attributes and actions) of the user objects to which it is providing access. However, different views of the same object, seen in different windows, may contain different subsets of UOM attributes and allow different subsets of actions to be performed.

5.1.3 Control

A control is an element of the user interface used to control the display, edit some value or start a command. Examples of user interface controls are a button, a scroll bar or a drop-down list. Controls need to be carefully selected to support the users' tasks.

5.1.4 State

A user interface can be in a state or mode. This is where a set of commands has a particular meaning based on the previous commands. So, a word processor could be in a page preview state where only some of the commands work the same way as in normal editing.

When designing the user interface it is important to try and minimise the different states that the user interface can be in and ensure that any states match the users' task points. It is also important to make sure that any state is clearly visible to the user and that it is clear how to get out of that state.

5.1.5 Style Guide

Style Guides are of great importance in projects to ensure a common look and feel across all facilities within the application. This can offer benefits to users who will become familiar with new applications more rapidly if the interface works in the same way in all contexts. If the same style guide is adopted across all applications, the training required in the use of new applications will be greatly reduced for those users already familiar with existing applications.

The use of a style guide can greatly accelerate a project for two reasons:

- the effort required in designing the user interface is reduced;

- commercially-available style guides sometimes contain component libraries which can be used to assemble a working user interface.

There are two main types of style guide:

- the Installation Style Guide, which sets broad standards for all applications within the organisation as a whole;

- the Application Style Guide, which is an elaboration of the Installation Style Guide for use on a particular project.

Ideally, the Installation Style Guide should be put in place before any project is initiated. In practice, the Installation Style Guide is often developed in parallel with the first application that is developed and is then adopted by subsequent projects.

Where specific user interface standards are to be used to develop the system, it is possible to purchase off-the-shelf style guides such as the Microsoft Windows Style Guide[3] and OSF Motif guide[4].

---

[3] see 'The Windows Interface, an Application Design Guide', Microsoft Press

[4] see 'OSF/Motif Style Guide', Revision 1.2, Prentice-Hall

All prototyping, screen design and report design should be carried out with reference to the style guide. It will help maintain standards throughout the organisation when considering the design of the interface.

A style guide should be utilised by the analysts and designers to provide information on the way standards will apply to the specification and design of dialogues and to the design of report formats.

5.2 Products of User Interface Design

The User Interface Design is a product of User Interface Design. It consists of the following:

- **Window Navigation Model**. This describes the window and dialogue structure and how the user navigates between them;

- **Window Specifications**. Each Window Specification is a description of one of the main windows and the views, states and actions it supports. This can be textual or within a prototype;

- **Help System Specification**. This is a specification of the help system and the procedures and topics that will be addressed by it.

These products are represented in Figure 5-3 and will be described in more detail in the following paragraphs.

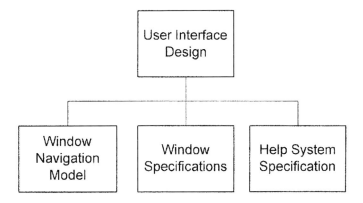

Figure 5-3 Product Breakdown Structure for User Interface Design

5.2.1 Window Navigation Model

Relationships between windows are documented by the Window Navigation Model. These relationships are driven by the needs of functions which support tasks. For complex functions it can be derived from the Function Navigation Models developed in Function Definition. A single Window Navigation Model is developed for the system as a whole based on individual functions. The constraints and controls required for specific functions will be built into the design and implementation of the final system.

A Window Navigation Model product can be produced in a variety of ways, including paper sketches, in a GUI prototyping tool, in textual description or in a CASE tool.

In general, navigation is about how users find the commands they need in a system. A Window Navigation Model is concerned with how the user opens new windows and transfers focus from one window to another. The Window Navigation Model does not show every possible way a user can move from one window to another. GUI environments usually allow multiple windows to be open at one time which the user can 'navigate' between without any formal control.

The aim of developing the Window Navigation Model is to:

- ensure that the window structure supports the user tasks;

- check that window navigation is minimised and users don't have to switch between different dialog boxes to get the information they need;

- ensure task completion points match up with the overall window structure;

- identify common dialogue structures and handle them in a consistent way;

- ensure functionality is placed where it is needed;

- ensure that exit points are provided for all transactions so users can cancel a transaction or put it on hold.

The Window Navigation Model defines the relationship between windows rather than their detailed content, which is described in the Window Specifications. However, some indication of content can be included to check that it can all be included in the window.

The Window Navigation Model should be developed to cover all main windows and dialog boxes. It should not include every message or help window. Any general-purpose navigation should be included in the Application Style Guide. The Window Navigation Model for a system can become very complex and difficult to maintain so it should be developed with care. The aim is to check that the system will 'hang together', that navigation is minimised and to look for overlaps and common areas of dialogue.

As explained above, the Window Navigation Model can be developed in a number of alternative ways. However, this volume will use one of the standard notation for a Window Navigation Model is shown in Figure 5-4.

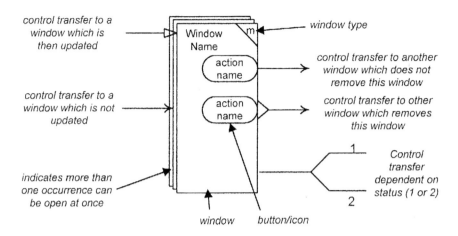

Figure 5-4 Notation for Window Navigation Model

Elements of the notation are as follows:

- a window is a rectangle containing the window's name. The window has an optional window type which is used as follows:

    - if left blank, the window is modeless, that is, the user can work in other windows without needing to respond to the dialog in this window;

    - an 'm' indicates the window is modal, that is, the user needs to complete the actions associated with that window before proceeding to another window[5].

- lines with arrows indicate control passing from one window to another. The shape of the arrow head indicates whether the window to which control is passed is updateable or non-updateable:

    - a closed arrow head ⟶▷ indicates that the next window can be updated;

    - an open arrow head ⟶→ indicates that the next window cannot be updated.

- window actions which transfer control to the next window are shown in ellipses from which the arrow to the next window box is sourced. An ellipse represents a feature of the interface that the user interacts with to effect the transfer to the next window - this would probably be a button or an icon;

---

[5] Note there is a difference between 'application modal' (user must respond to dialog before continuing to work in this application) and 'system modal' (user must respond before being able to do anything in this or any other application) but these are not distinguished in the notation.

- the transfer of control from a window can either remove the window from the interface or leave the window on the screen while control passes to another window. This is indicated on the line as it leaves the action box:

   - a triangle on the line represents the passing of control which removes the current window;

   - no triangle represents the passing of control which does not remove the current window.

- if the choice of the next window is dependent upon some status detected by the system, this can be indicated by a branching arrow where each branch is denoted with the status that caused it to be selected;

- if it is permissible to have several windows of the same type open at the same time, this is indicated by a series of 'shadow' boxes behind the window box.

An example of part of the Window Navigation Model taken from EU-Rent is shown in Figure 5-5.

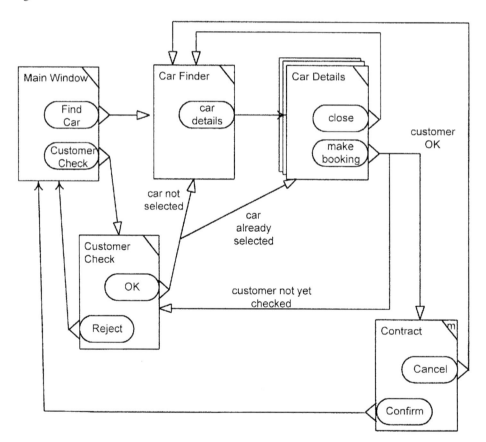

Figure 5-5 Window Navigation Model for Walk-in Rental

In this example the *Main Window* is firstly invoked. This has two controls *Find Car* and *Customer Check*. If either of these is taken then the *Main Window* is removed with the selected window being displayed. The *Car Finder* window can call up multiple instances of the *Car Details* window but is not removed when they are displayed. The window displays are carried forward until the *Contract* window is invoked where the user can either 'confirm' or 'cancel'. A confirm will take the user back to the starting window ready to accept the next Walk-in customer.

5.2.2 Window Specifications

A Window Specification is a detailed description of a window that will be used as the basis for the implementation of the window. Window Specifications can be developed at different levels of detail. For simple windows it is usually adequate to develop a rough hand-drawn sketch. For more complex, critical windows it is advised that the full specification detailed below is completed.

A hand-drawn sketch (story board) can be an extremely useful starting point in the development of a Window Specification as shown in Figure 5-6.

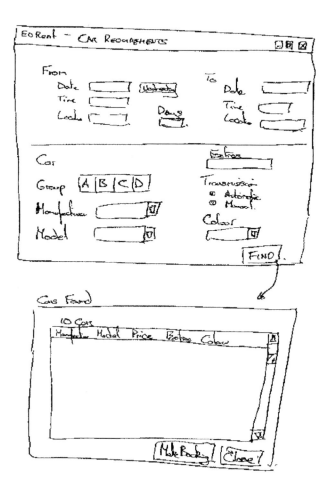

Figure 5-6 Example of hand-drawn sketch (story board) of windows for EU-Rent Car Finder

Hand-drawn sketches can be used to develop alternative specifications. For critical areas of the system, it is often useful to put together a prototype of a screen as part of the specification. A prototype for the EU-Rent Car finder window is shown in Figure 5-7.

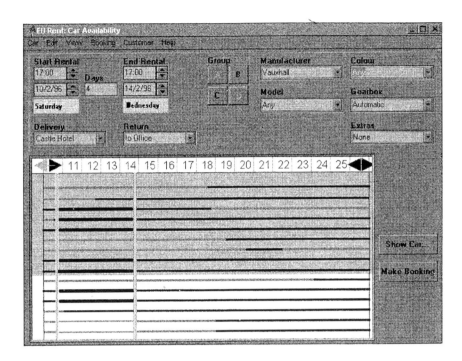

Figure 5-7 Prototype for the Car Finder window

In this example, the prototyped window has included more details than the hand-drawn sketch. The window includes the requirements of the customer as well as the available cars in summary form. The graph at the bottom of the window shows all available cars with the thicker lines representing cars that match the specified criteria. If the user selects one of these cars, another window will pop up and display details of the car.

In many cases, this will be an adequate level of detail for a Window Specification. However, for central and critical windows, it may be useful to develop more detailed written Window Specifications. These specifications can become extremely onerous to develop and maintain. Therefore only develop them to clarify complex windows.

A detailed Window Specification should describe the following features:

- window display, preferably in the form of a picture showing a sketch or prototype window design;

- window type (modality, number of instances, whether it can be resized);

- window title bar including: Window menu, title or how generated and window icons and menus;

- actions prior to displaying the window such as identifying any context that needs to be set, populating lists and defaults that are set;

- control behaviour that needs to be defined. Such as:

- type of list boxes, for example, whether they will allow single or multiple selection, how they will be populated, the sort order to be used, the expected number of items in the box;

- type of data entry fields, for example, whether they are mandatory or optional, field length, validation, routines, defaults, format where these features have not already been recorded in the Data Catalogue.

- behaviour a window supports once it has been displayed. It is often better to define this using a prototype supported by a textual document that describes any additional features that are not demonstrated in the prototype;

- view description detailing any views that are shown within a dialog box or window such as showing a form layout preview or a customer's previous contacts;

- messages generated from a dialog box can optionally be described together with tab sequences;

- help topic detailing the type of help and help on what. This might cross-reference the Help System Specification where appropriate;

- actions and behaviour that occur within the window or dialog box which are not described in the Application Style Guide. These should be described in an action table as illustrated in Figure 5-8.

Ref	User Action	Condition	Success Outcome	Failure Outcome
22.1.	Date of birth entered	Driver between 20 and 70 years	Enable move to next field	Message indicating rental not permitted without additional insurance.
22.2.	OK button pressed	All fields have been validated	Print form dialog	Indicate problem and move cursor to field in error.

Figure 5-8 Example of action table

5.2.3 Help System Specification

The help system and documentation need to be defined when the functionality is sufficiently stable.

The Help System Specification should include the following:

- procedures that should be described in the help system;

- concepts that should be explained in the help system;

- field and dialog help (field-level help may be included in the Data Catalogue).

Help should be defined for the different audiences of the system and should be developed by technical writers with experience in help system development. There are two different types of help, un-requested help, such as messages that indicate what a function will do in a status bar, and user requested help.

User requested help needs to be built from an understanding of the users' tasks. It must ensure that it answers real questions and uses words that end-users will understand.

5.3 The User Interface Design Technique

The activities of User Interface Design are as follows and are illustrated in Figure 5-9:

- agree style guide;

- design windows in outline;

- design window navigation model;

- specify windows in detail.

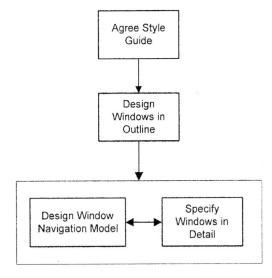

Figure 5-9 Activities of User Interface Design

As can be seen from this diagram, Window Specifications and the Window Navigation Model are developed in parallel as one will affect the other. These activities are described further below.

5.3.1 Agree style guide

At all times during the design of the user interface the relevant style guide should be referred to. A Style Guide should be regarded as a set of standards to be followed by the project. It is advisable for an installation to have a set of standards for all projects, the Installation Style Guide. This is adapted and expanded to ensure that project-specific standards can also be defined. The project-specific style guide is called the Application Style Guide.

For GUI-based systems, there is often a commercially-available style guide[6] for the specific technology selected for the interface. Where possible, the interface should adhere very closely to its commercial style guide so that users of different applications will be presented with a consistent interface. In addition to the commercial style guide, it will be necessary to write more detailed style guidance specific to the Organisation (Installation Style Guide) or application being developed (Application Style Guide).

This guidance serves to document agreement on common standards that will be followed throughout the design. Where common dialog boxes or common task sequences can be identified these should be documented together with detailed agreement on terminology and use of controls.

The menu and toolbar design should be included in the Application Style Guide. This should describe the order and structure of the menu bar, menus and any sub-menus. Each menu item should indicate the menu label and what will be invoked by it. Similarly, any toolbars that will be provided should be described.

The Application Style Guide should take into account the results of User Analysis (see Work Practice Modelling chapter) with particular reference to the User Class Descriptions. The style of the user interface needs to be tailored towards the capabilities and experience of the users. In many cases, the interface will be designed to be 'all-purpose' and usable by all user classes. For applications with larger user populations where user needs are more polarised, there may be a need to provide different styles of user interface for different groups of users.

5.3.2 Design windows in outline

As a precursor to defining windows, it is necessary to define the views of user objects required for each function.

A view of an object presents the information and functionality that a user needs in support of an on-line function. In Function Definition, the function is cross-referenced to the user objects and actions from the User Object Model required for that function. There may be more than one view of a user object required for a single function, however, and this needs to be defined. In designing the windows to support a function, we are interested in how the user will actually interact with these views.

The default will be that for a particular function, there will be one view per user object. The same view of a user object may be re-used in different functions. However, in some

---

[6] Examples are the OSF/Motif Style Guide, IBM's Common User Access and Microsoft's 'The Windows Interface Guidelines for Software Design', 1995.

cases, it will be preferable to provide multiple views of the same object for the following reasons:

- there is a large amount of information which would be more easy to understand if it were broken down;

- the information that is most frequently used could be presented in a different view from that which is less frequently used;

- where the information is complex, it may be useful to allow the user to view it in different ways, possibly summarised or graphically presented;

- views should present the user with the most appropriate view of the information to facilitate decision making;

- views may vary depending upon what actions the user is likely (or constrained) to use in a particular context;

- different user roles may have different levels of access permitted to the information.

Once the views have been decided, each view of a user object should be allocated to a pane in a window. Some views are required together and others will not need to be seen at the same time. A user interface is most flexible if each window consists of one or more views of a single object.

It helps at this stage to sketch out roughly the windows for a function, either as a brief description or as actual hand-drawn sketches showing how the various elements of the window might fit together. An example of a rough initial sketch is shown in Figure 5-10. This is only an initial view. When the Window Navigation Model and detailed Window Specification are constructed, the design of the window may need to change significantly. Also, the design of windows is rarely considered complete until prototyping and evaluation have been performed (see Chapter 6) .

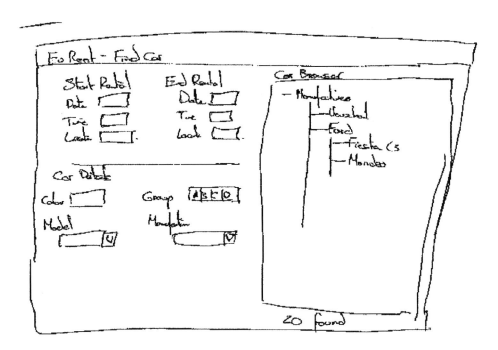

Figure 5-10 Example rough outline sketch of a window

5.3.3 Design Window Navigation Model

Before the Window Navigation Model can be designed, it is necessary to review the windowing structures supported by the environment and decide on the most appropriate windowing structure to use. This information should be defined in the Installation Style Guide. For example:

- use a tiled windowing structure with no overlapping windows where users are performing time critical actions with a well-defined task structure such as a call centre or an information monitoring role;

- use overlapping windows where users need to compare information and there will be a dynamic task sequence;

- provide a tabbed window structure where users frequently need to switch between defined 'pages' in the application.

When the overall windowing style for the application has been selected based on the users' tasks the window structure and navigation actions can be defined for each function.

Start from the main window and for each function map out the window sequence to support the task structure. Where a Function Navigation Model has been completed, this should be used as the starting point. The development of a Window Navigation Model from a Function Navigation Model does not follow a set of rules. Several function elements can be combined into one window or a single function element could be split across multiple windows. One factor to bear in mind is that windows should be re-usable wherever possible so common function elements may be better implemented using separate windows. Also, navigation between windows must support the associations between user objects

The Function Navigation Model for the Walk-in Rental function is shown in Figure 5-11.

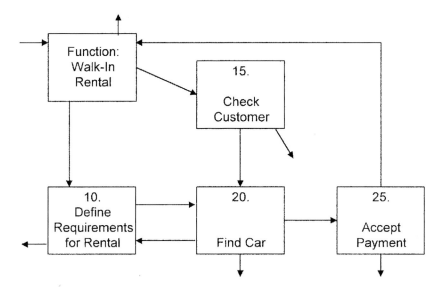

Figure 5-11 Function Navigation Model for Walk-in Rental function

This is translated into a Window Navigation Model as shown in Figure 5-12.

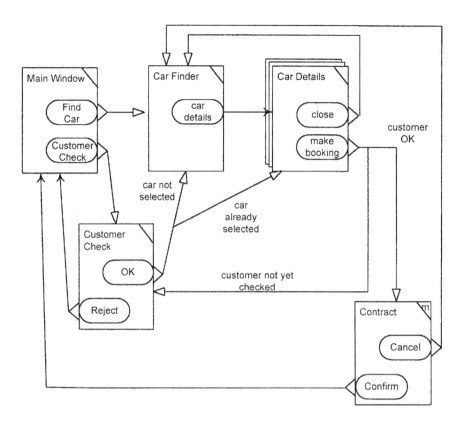

Figure 5-12 Window Navigation Model for Walk-in Rental

It can be seen from this example that the function elements Define Requirements for Rental and Find Car have been combined into a single window Car Finder. The Accept Payment function element has been incorporated into the Contract window. To allow additional flexibility, the Check Customer part of the function can now be entered once the car has been selected, but the controls specified in the Function Definition are enforced as the dialog cannot proceed until the Customer Check has been completed.

Having mapped out the window structure it should be reviewed to identify:

- common dialog boxes;
- how the sequence can be simplified by combining windows.

5.3.4 Specify windows in detail

Window Specifications are produced for all major windows to a varying degree of detail depending upon complexity. Windows are designed following the sequence of activities shown in Figure 5-13.

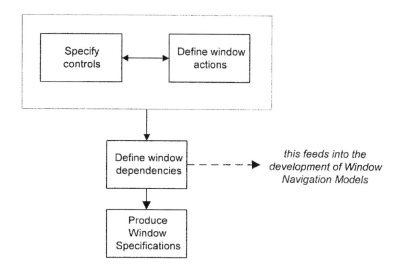

Figure 5-13 Activities in definition of windows

These activities are described as follows:

- **Specify controls**. Where a user is able to enter or amend information, controls will be required. Some of these controls will be enforced by the event processing within the Conceptual Model but other controls will need to be enforced at the user interface. Where a screen attribute can have only one of a set of valid values, the interface should present only that set from which the user can select one. Formats and lengths can be enforced at the user interface. Protected fields should be obvious to the users so they do not attempt to alter their value;

- **Define window actions**. It is necessary to ensure that the windows presented to the user for a particular function contain all the actions required to allow the user to successfully complete the function. There may be a number of general actions available as well as a specific one defined in the User Object Model views for the function;

- **Define window dependencies**. The definition of navigation between windows requires first an understanding of the dependencies and permitted/possible sequences between windows;

- **Produce Window Specifications**. The product of window design is a Window Specification. This defines the details of the window including window title and detailed design, possibly including a detailed prototype of the window.

5.4 Relationship with other techniques

Below is a list of other analysis and design techniques with which User Interface Design interfaces. A brief description is listed together with a reference to where the reader can find a full description of the technique.

5.4.1 User Object Modelling (see Chapter 3)

User objects are the elements of the user interface with which the user interacts. The User Object Model is therefore a very important input to User Interface Design. Windows are based on user objects and the navigation between windows must support the associations between user objects.

5.4.2 Function Definition (see Chapter 4)

Functions are the automated facilities provided by the IT application to support the users' tasks. Functions therefore provide the bridge between Task Modelling and User Interface Design. Function Navigation Models provide the basis for the Window Navigation Model.

5.4.3 Prototyping and Evaluation (see Chapter 6)

Prototyping and Evaluation are a necessary part of User Interface design. The initial windows and navigation designed using the techniques and products described in this chapter need to be brought to life and demonstrated to users to ensure that they meet their requirements.

5.4.4 Work Practice Modelling (see Chapter 2)

User Interface Design must support the tasks of the user. This means that the whole of User Interface Design is influenced by the products of Work Practice Modelling.

6   PROTOTYPING AND EVALUATION

A prototype is a model or example used to help envisage the finished article during the design process. Prototyping can take a number of different forms and can be used for several different purposes. Some types of prototype are treated as initial versions of the system which are iteratively refined into the delivered system. Other types of prototype are used for a particular purpose and then thrown away.

Within this chapter, prototyping is taken to have three principal purposes:

- to establish requirements for the new system;

- to help develop the User Interface Design;

- to demonstrate the usability of a User Object Model and other design products.

With the increasing use of Graphical User Interfaces (GUIs), prototyping is becoming more of an integral part of any project and therefore the main emphasis of this chapter is in the use of prototyping and evaluation in GUI Design.

Within this chapter, Prototyping is taken to be the techniques for developing a 'prototype' which will be demonstrated to the users. Evaluation is taken to be the technique of actually demonstrating the prototype to the users.Although Prototyping and Evaluation are defined here, as part of the design of the user interface, it can be used at all stages of a development project and can even be a very useful tool in finding out the basic requirements for the new system.

The place of GUI prototyping and Evaluation in the System Development Template is shown in Figure 6-1.

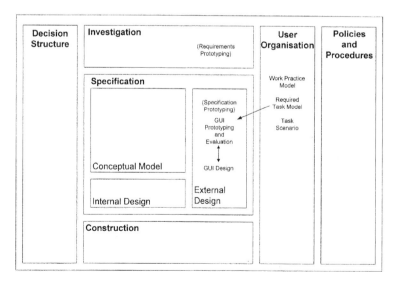

Figure 6-1 Prototyping in the System Development Template

GUI prototyping is concerned with developing a working example of the user interface that users can interact with. It is iterative and involves the user in evaluating the user interface.

Evaluation involves the setting of the prototyping scope and assessing the results of the prototype. It is an important part of the overall prototyping process as it establishes what changes are required to the user interface as a result of prototyping. The objectives of evaluation are to identify usability problems, to assess whether the GUI design satisfies specified usability requirements and to evaluate whether the GUI design will be usable in practice by its intended users.

Prototyping the user interface and evaluating it with users is a vital part of the process. Early prototyping can help save costly mistakes by clarifying assumptions and validating requirements. However, care is needed when developing early user interface prototypes to manage users' expectations on development timescales and functionality.

As prototyping and evaluation are process-based rather than product-based, there is minimal description of the products of prototyping in this chapter. The principal product of the process is the prototype itself and this can take many forms dependent upon the implementation environment being used.

An area of prototyping that is extremely useful in practice but which is not covered in detail in this chapter is the prototyping of reports. Sketching out the proposed layouts of reports and showing them to users is a very effective way of ensuring that the content and layout of reports will meets the users' needs.

User interfaces need to be prototyped to:

- validate and refine requirements early in the process when changes are less costly;

- resolve design uncertainty about whether a specific design meets user needs;

- explore the dynamic properties of a user interface which cannot be properly represented on paper;

- provide an effective means of communicating the vision and scope of the system to users and other parts of the project team.

Evaluation is a process which aims to check that the system matches the needs of the user.

6.1   Concepts of Prototyping and Evaluation

6.1.1 Types of GUI prototype

There is often an underlying assumption that prototypes should aim to be presented on screens to users, preferably with a wide scope, reasonable fidelity and enough functionality to 'convince' a user that this could be real. However, this approach has two main disadvantages:

- this type of prototype can be relatively costly to develop and takes a significant amount of time;

- the closer the prototype looks to the 'real thing' the more difficult it is to keep the user's expectations realistic and to make the user concentrate on the issues being addressed by the prototype.

Consideration should be given to using more 'low-tech' prototypes which can, with some effort, achieve the same results as automated prototypes but quicker, cheaper and with fewer problems with user expectations. The analyst can use paper prototypes or story boards to 'walk through' an area of the design. These are low fidelity prototypes with simulated data and functionality. An example of this type of prototype is shown in Figure 6-2.

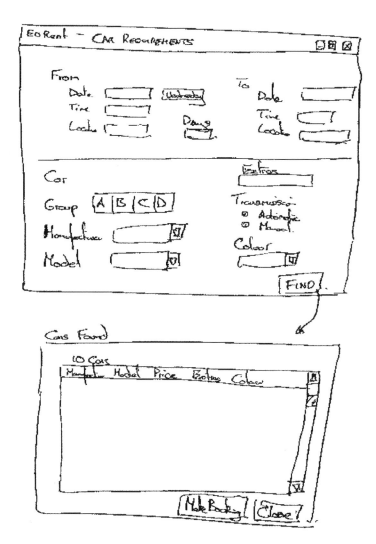

Figure 6-2 Example of low fidelity paper prototype

An example of a high fidelity prototype in the same area is shown in Figure 6-3.

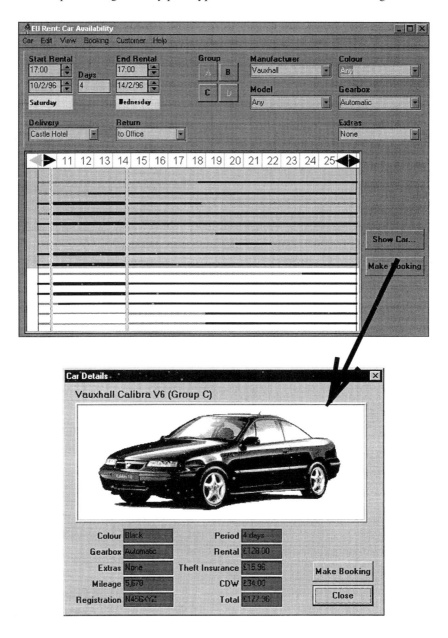

Figure 6-3 High fidelity prototype

Another type of prototype is a navigation prototype. This shows roughly how different windows may follow on from one another. An example of a roughly sketched navigation prototype is shown in Figure 6-4.

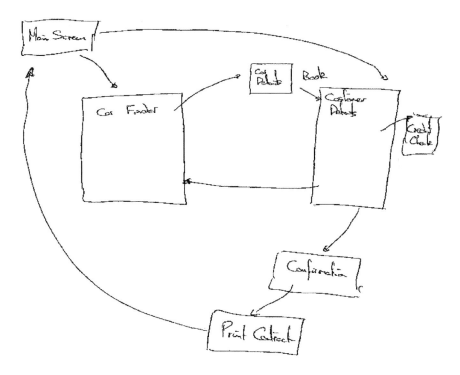

Figure 6-4 Roughly sketched navigation prototype

6.1.2 Considerations in Prototyping and Evaluation

Deciding between a demonstration or user driven prototype

The aim of GUI prototyping is to learn what the problems are with the design and how users will operate with the new system. It can prove very useful if the prototype can be designed so as to give users control of driving the prototype so that the analyst can learn what mistakes users make and where they have difficulties.

Where the purpose of the prototype is to gain acceptance or present current work to a number of people it may be more appropriate to demonstrate the prototype.

Things to manage when showing a prototype to users

The following aspects need to be carefully managed when showing a prototype to users:

- users' impressions of the project – if the user sees something working, it is difficult to explain why the system will take a lot longer to develop in full. Conversely, if the prototype does not have a particularly attractive interface, users can form a negative impression of progress;

- it is very important to make it clear to users and sponsors what the purpose of the prototype is. Often users can feel that it is they that are being evaluated – it is the design that is being evaluated not the abilities of the users;

- ease of making changes. It is not always obvious how much development effort will be required to implement changes. Before any change is agreed, there should be some (broad) estimate of effort required to implement the change which can be balanced against the perceived benefit of the change. If a 'nice to have' change will be very costly, the user may decide to drop the requirement;

- timescales for further development. Individual changes may be small but taken overall the timescales for development might be affected. Again, care should be taken when agreeing changes to the specification;

- the user should be asked to justify the business benefits of any significant change.

Key points to bear in mind

In planning and developing prototypes, the following points should be kept in mind:

- benefits of prototyping can be gained at any point in a project. It is useful to consider prototyping and evaluation at an early stage in the project. Also, prototypes can be developed when problems are encountered – a prototype can help move a project forward;

- the developer should not consider him/ herself to be a representative model of the user – at all times, concentration should be on what the user needs and what the user finds usable;

- it is very important to control the iterative nature of prototyping and evaluation. Before a prototyping exercise is started, the project should be clear as to what is expected to be achieved – once the goal of the exercise is reached it should be stopped.

6.2   Properties of GUI prototypes

Features of different prototypes can vary in a number of important ways. It is important that an appropriate type of prototype can be chosen to best suit the purposes of the prototype.

There are a number of different properties of GUI prototypes that can vary as follows:

- scope;

- fidelity;

- functionality.

These are described in more detail in the following paragraphs.

6.2.1 Scope

The scope of a prototype defines how much or how little of the user interface design is prototyped. A prototype can vary between having a narrow scope and having a wide scope. This is illustrated in Figure 6-5.

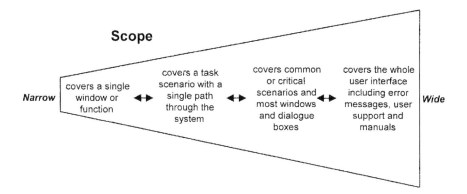

Figure 6-5 Scope of GUI prototypes

A prototype with a narrow scope may focus on a complex window which is causing users problems. A prototype with wide scope may look at navigation around the whole system.

Where a system is to be incrementally developed using prototyping, the scope might change with time starting with a narrow scope and over time expanding towards the full (wide) scope.

6.2.2 Fidelity

The fidelity of a prototype is the degree to which the prototype is detailed or realistic. A prototype can vary between being of low fidelity and being of high fidelity. This is illustrated in Figure 6-6.

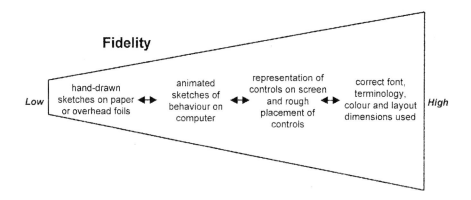

Figure 6-6 Fidelity of GUI prototypes

A low fidelity prototype may be hand-drawn sketches used to validate requirements. A high fidelity prototype would use the correct colours, fonts and would position all items with the right separation in a window. This might be used to validate the Application Style Guide.

Where the prototype is simply being used to drive out requirements then we would expect the fidelity to be low. Where the prototype is being used as part of the implementation then we would expect the fidelity to be high.

6.2.3 Functionality

The functionality of a prototype is the degree to which the data appearing on the screen and functionality is 'working' or 'live' or how much is simulated. This is illustrated in Figure 6-7.

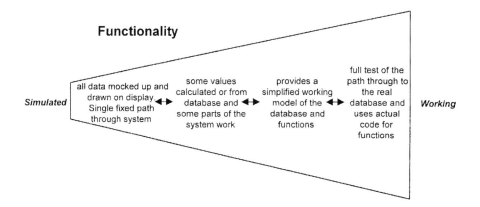

Figure 6-7 Functionality of GUI prototypes

Simulated functionality can be used to test design concepts and working functionality may be used to test the usability of the system and to allow users more choice when using a prototype.

6.3   GUI Prototyping and Evaluation Procedure

Figure 6-8 illustrates a typical approach to prototyping and evaluation. The main process of prototyping and evaluation is iterative and can be repeated as many times as necessary to achieve the objectives of the prototyping exercise.

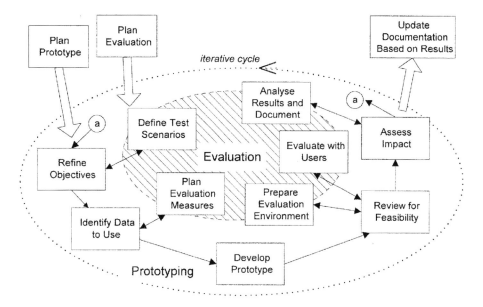

Figure 6-8 Prototyping and Evaluation

The activities of prototyping (the development of the prototype) and evaluation (the demonstration of the developed prototype to the users) operate together and are dependent on one another. They should be planned and executed in parallel with one another.

6.3.1 Developing the prototype

The activities of prototyping shown in Figure 6-8 are listed here and described further in the following paragraphs:

- plan prototype;
- refine objectives;
- identify data to use; develop prototype;

- review for feasibility;

- assess impact to the prototype;

- update documentation based on results.

As a general consideration, developers should avoid the temptation to make fixes or change the prototype during prototyping and evaluation sessions. Any changes to prototypes should be made in a controlled way and on the basis of considered evaluation. However, it is sometimes useful to design a prototype where parts of the user interface can be changed dynamically, especially where the aim of the prototype is to get the user to sign up to the screen design.

Plan Prototype

This activity takes place before the iterative cycle of prototyping.

A prototype needs clearly defined objectives and scope. The objectives are set by determining what you want to learn or achieve with the prototype. It is important to understand the objectives and scope before prototyping is commenced as this will help in the management of prototyping and limit the number of iterations.

Far too many prototypes fail to achieve anything because the analysts and the users have never agreed a common agenda for the prototyping exercise.

GUI prototypes should be based on task scenarios rather than concentrating on a particular function or doing a superficial prototype of the whole system. By walking through a scenario, users will be able to confirm that the system fits in with the overall set of tasks and meets their requirements in the context of their jobs.

The overall scope of the prototype will be influenced by the objectives of the prototyping exercise and how the prototype will be presented or evaluated by users. The scope of the prototype should reflect one or more Task Scenarios that the prototype should support. These scenarios should be carefully selected to cover the design features of interest.

Figure 6-9 gives some examples of objectives that may be set for specific projects and indicates their influence on the scope of the prototyping exercise.

Example objectives	Prototyping technique
Refine requirements for functionality, key task sequences and user support.	Design alternatives as rough paper or overhead prototypes. Wide scope, low fidelity and simulated functionality.
Refine style guide	High fidelity prototype of key parts of the design to ensure it can be implemented with the selected development tool.
Validate User Object Model	Low fidelity paper prototype of major parts of system.
Validate Required Task Models and navigation	Low fidelity wide scope prototypes of major windows showing navigation features.
Build acceptance for work of project with users.	Animated high fidelity prototype with single path through.
Determine how a complex window will work	Functional prototype of window with sufficient support for scenarios. This will be low scope, high fidelity and probably high functionality.
Check that design will achieve usability goals	Detailed prototype that allows goals to be tested. Scope will be determined by the number and type of goals and will usually have high fidelity and high functionality.
Select between design alternatives	A suitably high fidelity prototype of the alternative designs.
Ensure that a specific task is properly supported.	Prototype with scope to support task – whether low or high fidelity unimportant
Ensure that design changes have solved identified problems	Prototype with design changes implemented from a previous prototype

Figure 6-9 Example objectives and their influence on the prototyping scope

It is also important to plan the number of iterations that will occur with the prototype and define a timebox[7] for their development. For example, a paper prototype may be limited to three iterations over four days. In some cases, it may not be possible to predict how many iterations will be required. In these cases, it is necessary to define a stopping condition, that is, a recognisable state that will indicate that the prototyping exercise has met its objectives and can be discontinued.

When planning the prototyping process it is also important to define what you expect to be able to carry forward from the prototype. With low cost prototypes it is important to learn the lessons from the prototype and then throw the prototypes away. With more detailed prototypes, it is possible that those parts of the prototype that are successful can be developed further into the working system.

Selecting prototyping tools

As part of the planning process, it is necessary to determine what prototyping tools are going to be used. It is usually preferable to select tools that are able to simulate the interface that the user will see in the finished system. For some types of prototype a new simulation environment may need to be constructed. The prototyping tools need to be selected based on the objectives of the prototype and the stage in the project.

---

[7] A 'timebox' involves setting a deadline by which an objective will be met, not necessarily defining precisely the content of the work that will be completed by the deadline.

Tools should be selected based on a number of factors including the following:

- speed of iteration;

- match to the target environment;

- portability into a working system;

- learning time;

- support for the design task;

- cost.

If a similar system exists which has a user interface similar to the one being prototyped then it may be useful to use it as the basis for the prototyping exercise. This has the advantage that the users will already be familiar with parts of the interface and the disadvantage that the old system may not be written in the best medium for developing a prototype.

Refine objectives

Before starting each iteration of the prototype it is important to review the objectives for this iteration and to define the scope of the prototype. For the first iteration, this should simply be a confirmation of the objectives and scope set for the whole prototyping exercise. However, subsequent iterations may require a change to the scope depending upon the outcome of the previous iteration.

Identify data to use

The data used in the prototype should be as realistic as possible so that users accept the prototype. The use of realistic data will also demonstrate that the issues are well understood by the analysts. Unless the data is realistic, discussions are likely to focus on the content of the data rather than the features of the user interface.

The creation of data for prototyping can be extremely labour-intensive. If conversion of data from the current system is relatively straightforward, it may be best to use real data, possibly with slight modifications if security is an issue. In this case, care should be taken to select data instances that contain sufficient variety to demonstrate the features of the prototype in a meaningful way.

Develop prototype

In many Organisations, an Installation Style Guide may exist. The existence of such a style guide should be established and a copy obtained for direct reference in the development of prototypes. Where the Installation Style Guide is very general, it is necessary to develop a specific style guide that can be used during the prototyping exercise. Preferably, any style guide used during prototyping should be the style guide that is used for the implemented system.

If tools conforming to existing standards (such as Microsoft Windows [8], OSF/Motif [9], etc.) are to be used to build the user interface, it is possible to purchase off-the-shelf style guides, some of which have component libraries that can be used directly to build prototypes.

Early prototypes can be built rapidly using paper, and then later prototypes can switch to using higher fidelity prototyping tools which can also demonstrate functionality.

Review for feasibility

The prototype should go through a brief review for feasibility before any evaluation with users. It is important that users are not given expectations of performance and functionality that will be difficult to meet in the developed system. This is less important for low fidelity prototypes where users will accept that a hand-drawn sketch of the design is still subject to change. However, the importance increases as the prototypes becomes more realistic. One of the biggest dangers of prototyping is that the users are given the impression that the system is nearly complete – managing the users expectations is one of the most important parts of managing the prototyping exercise.

Assess impact of changes to the prototype

Once the prototype has been evaluated with the users and the results of the evaluation analysed, it is necessary to assess the impact of any proposed changes to the prototype/user interface design in terms of the amount of work required, benefits vs. costs and how long the changes will take to implement. Where a formal assessment of the impact is required, an impact report should be prepared.

The results of the evaluation need to be considered and priorities for changes to the original prototype identified. The importance of each change should be balanced against the effort required to make the change.

Update documentation based on results

Once the total prototyping exercise has been completed, it is necessary to update any relevant documentation that has been impacted, particularly investigation and specification products such as the Requirements Catalogue or Required Task Models.

6.3.2 Evaluation

Evaluation is the technique that is used to check that the system matches the needs of the users. The evaluation process is closely linked with the user interface prototyping process where it is generally used to check that the usability requirements are being met.

---

[8] See 'The Windows@ Interface Guidelines for Software Design',1995, Microsoft Press.

[9] See 'OSF/Motif Style Guide, Revision 2.0', 1995, Prentice-Hall.

The activities of Evaluation shown in Figure 6-8 are listed here and described further in the following paragraphs:

- plan evaluation;

- define test scenarios;

- plan evaluation measures;

- prepare evaluation environment;

- evaluate with users;

- analyse results and document.

Plan evaluation

This activity involves planning the evaluation process and selecting representative users who match the identified user roles and classes to test the prototype. Depending on the type of evaluation and the validity of the results required, between eight and fifteen users should be actively involved in the evaluation of the system. The evaluation process needs to be carefully controlled if it is going to produce valid and repeatable results. Where evaluation is being used to identify problems in the design a less formal approach can be used. The evaluation sessions are an important project milestone and need to be planned well in advance to ensure that the appropriate users are available and can participate.

Figure 6-10 gives some examples of objectives that may be set for specific projects and indicates their influence on the type of evaluation technique used.

Example objectives	Evaluation technique
Refine requirements for functionality, key task sequences and user support.	User focus groups to discuss the designs or JAD[9] workshops.
Refine style guide	Review of document and prototype to get user comments.
Validate User Object Model	User walkthrough of the design where users are given common tasks to perform.
Validate Required Task Models and navigation	Check tasks are complete and coherent
Build acceptance for work of project with users.	Demonstrate system to users and explain benefits and timescales. Carry out standardised survey of user needs.
Determine how a complex window will work	Test that users working through a scenario can use the complex window.
Check that design will achieve usability goals	Detailed usability test that checks the usability metrics set in the usability requirements.
Select between design alternatives	Test scenarios which work through alternative designs and measure against usability requirements
Ensure that a specific task is properly supported.	Check that the task can be performed within performance criteria.
Ensure that design changes have solved identified problems	Evaluate that the design changes solve problems and do not introduce further problems.

Figure 6-10 Example of objectives

Other evaluation techniques that can be used are:

- expert review where an expert in user interface design can be brought in to review an early prototype and comment on problems they have identified. This can be used in addition to testing and observing users to give early insight into likely problems;

- user surveys or structured interviews can be carried out to collect users' subjective reactions to their existing system and then to the prototype system. Care needs to be exercised in ensuring that the questions are standardised and not biased.

Define test scenarios

It is probable that the scenarios used for prototyping will be a selection of Task Scenarios developed as part of Task Modelling (see the Work Practice Modelling chapter). The scenarios and data used need to be selected to match the objectives of the prototype. The sequence of the user tasks needs to be carefully defined together with any training that may be given. This will produce an overall test script which will include:

- instructions to the participants;

- any training or demonstrations provided;

- task scenarios for user to work through;

- follow-up questions.

Plan evaluation measures

The evaluation measures selected need to be based on the type of prototype and the stage in the project. An existing system may be evaluated to provide baseline performance data for identifying improvements. However, for an early paper prototype the main aim is to identify areas where users had problems or the system failed to match their expectations. For a more functional prototype it may be useful to include measures such as task completion time and time in an error state.

Prepare evaluation environment

The evaluation environment needs to be considered with care so that evaluation can take place without interruptions in a place that is non-threatening to users.

Evaluate with users

The evaluation session needs to be piloted first to test out the procedures and check that they will be providing the results intended. The pilot can be run with someone from the team who is unfamiliar with the design rather than an actual user.

The actual sessions can then be run with the intended users and the data collected. Care must be taken to ensure that users are not overly influenced by the evaluator and that they do not bring preconceived prejudices into the evaluation to help ensure that the session produces useful results. It is likely that the evaluation sessions will last a couple of hours and will need support from the following roles:

- **Evaluator**. This person is likely to sit with the user to answer any questions and prompt them to think aloud when they are having problems to explain what is causing difficulty. They should be careful not to prompt or lead the user.

- **Assistant**. The assistant will record critical incidents and comments the user makes and may also operate any video or recording equipment. If it is felt to be useful, tools can be used to capture keystrokes.

Analyse results and document

The results of the evaluation can be analysed in a number of different ways. The detailed notes kept during prototyping sessions can be written up into a brief report which summarises:

- good and bad points of the design;
- comments made by users;
- printout of the user interface with problem areas marked;
- prioritised list of problems;
- any performance or error metrics.

Once the evaluation has been concluded changes to the design need to be agreed and documented and these can feed into the next prototype or provide input to the

Requirements Specification. The aim must be to identify improvements that have direct business benefit by improving the usability of the system.

6.4 Relationship with other analysis and design techniques

Below is a list of other analysis and design techniques with which Prototyping and Evaluation interfaces. A brief description is listed together with a reference to where the reader can find a full description of the technique.

6.4.1 User Interface Design (covered in Chapter 5)

User Interface Design and prototyping are closely connected with one another. The user interface can be designed initially using User Interface Design techniques but it needs to be prototyped and evaluated before it can be considered stable. Thus, the user interface should be developed iteratively or in parallel using design and prototyping to build on one another.

6.4.2 Work Practice Modelling (covered in Chapter 2)

Work Practice Modelling provides the definition of users' tasks which are to be supported by dialogues. The scope of individual prototypes would normally be based upon Task Scenarios.

6.4.3 Requirements Definition (covered in The Business Context volume)

New requirements may be uncovered by prototyping and evaluation or requirements may need to be modified.

7   META-MODEL FOR GUI DESIGN

The purpose of the concepts Meta-models contained within this chapter is to explain the concepts of the method in order to establish a common understanding between all parties interested in using and interpreting the method. The models attempts to identify the key concepts of User Centred Design and shows the interrelationships between the concepts.

There are two Meta-models presented here. The first one (Figure 7-1) covers Work Practice Modelling. The second one covers the rest of User Centred Design. Each model is presented with descriptions for each of the concepts.

7.1   Meta-model for Work Practice Modelling

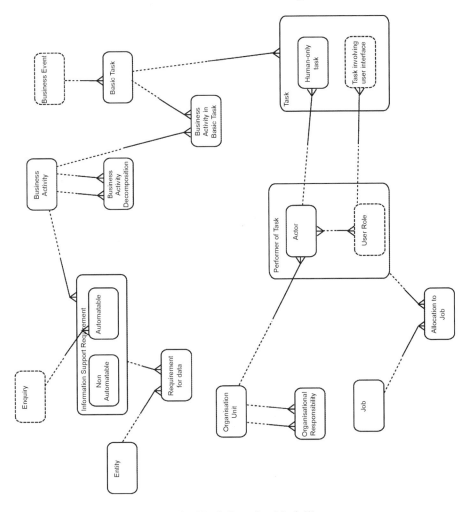

Figure 7-1 Model of concepts for Work Practice Modelling

Concept	Description
Actor	Actors can be identified as a collection of proposed job holders who will share a large proportion of common tasks whether using the IT system or not. Actors will often be identified by defining coherent sets of business activities which will be performed by the same people.
Basic Task	The complete set of business activities triggered by a single business event irrespective of who or what is to perform the business activities.
Business Activity	A transformation in the business system which acts on inputs to produce outputs. Business activities can be dependent on other business activities, they can be triggered by business events and are performed by actors in the business system. Business activities can be broken down hierarchically into component business activities.
Business Activity Decomposition	Relationship between two business activities whereby one is part of the decomposition of the other.
Business Event	A happening in the business context to which the business system has to react. It will always be associated with a trigger which activates one or more business activities. It may be the source of events to which the automated system needs to respond.
Enquiry	A type of trigger to a Conceptual Model process which causes one or more entities/entity aspects to be accessed but not updated.
Entity	Something, whether concrete or abstract, which is of relevance to the system and about which information needs to be stored. This concept represents a general definition of the entity that can be shared by a number of different systems/areas. It is an aspect of the entity that is represented within a specific project's Logical Data Model.
Human-only Task	A type of task that needs to be done by the user without support from the computer.
Information Support Requirement	The Business Activity Model represents a system of business activities which will be supported by an information system. The information system covers all the stored information that is needed by business activities and can contain non-automated information sources as well as IT support. A requirement for information support identifies the need for specific information required to execute a particular business activity. Automatable requirements are likely to identify requirements for enquiries from the new system.
Organisational Responsibility	A concept representing the hierarchy of organisational units. Each organisational unit at a higher level has responsibility for units defined at the level below.
Organisation Unit	An organisational grouping within which staff responsibilities and tasks are defined. Hierarchically decomposed. At the lowest level, individuals or roles are defined.
Task	A task is a connected subset of business activities triggered by a business event and undertaken by an actor or user role.
Task Involving User Interface	A type of task that needs to be done by the user in conjunction with the computer.
User Role	User roles are derived with reference to actors – they are the subset of actors who require a user interface to the automated system. User roles might be organised slightly differently from actors as they can be defined as groups of users who will require access to the same sets of functions with the same level of authority.
Job	A coherent set of activities undertaken within the business environment undertaken by a set of actors/user roles.

7.2 Meta-model for User Object Modelling, Function Definition, User Interface Design and Prototyping and Evaluation

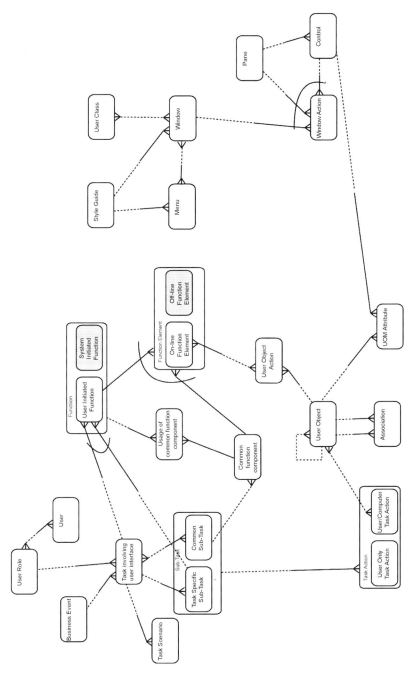

Figure 7-2 Concepts diagram for User Centred Design

Concept	Description
Business Event	A happening in the business context to which the business system has to react. The reason for initiating an event-driven task.
Common Function Component	A discrete piece of processing which can be re-used in a number of different functions. Common sub-tasks will almost always require support from one or more common function components.
Common Sub-task	The description of a discrete sub-task which is used in more sub-task than one Task Model. Common tasks should form the basis for re-use of function components from the External Design which has the advantage of reducing development effort and improving consistency of style as presented to the users.
Control	A control is an element of the user interface used to control the display, edit some value or start a command. Examples of user interface controls are a button, a scroll bar or a drop-down list. Controls need to be carefully selected to support the user's task.
Function	A packaging of all elements of process definition which are required to support a task/sub-task or an off-line facility of the system.
Menu	The means by which a user is able to select and invoke the user dialogues associated with functions.
Off-line Function Element	That part of a function which has no interaction with the user. Instead, the data is input as a batch or series of batches, the whole of the database processing for the function element is completed by the system and outputs (usually reports) are generated by the system.
On-line Function Element	That part of a function where the user and system interact to complete the processing for the function via the use of a dialogue. This will require the provision of a user-computer interface.
Pane	Part of a window through which the user can interact with user objects.
Style Guide	A Style Guide describes the conventions and guidelines to be adopted when developing an application's user interface.
Sub-task	A discrete part of a task or other sub-task. Sub-tasks form the hierarchy within a Required Task Model.
System initiated function	A type of function which is time-triggered or initiated by some condition that can be detected by the system. This type of function would be expected to run without any user intervention.
Task involving user interface	A piece of work that needs to be done by the user in conjunction with the computer. This type of task is performed by a user role in response to a business event.
Task Action	An element of a task or sub-task. Task actions are used to derive user object actions.
Task Scenario	A Task Scenario is a concrete example of a specific task which provides a complete story, or business thread.
Task specific sub-task	A type of sub-task which belongs to a single task and is not re-used in any other task.
UOM Attribute	An element of a user object as defined by the user. A UOM attribute may be equivalent to attributes in the Logical Data Model.
User Class	A subset of the total user population of the required system who are similar in terms of their frequency of use, relevant knowledge and personal experience. The user interface needs to be designed to suit the user classes of the target user population.
User Object	Something the user will want to recognise as a component of the user interface of the automated system
User Object Action	A user object action is a requirement to manipulate, view or change a user object.

Concept	Description
User-initiated function	A type of function which is initiated by some type of user action. The function can contain elements of on-line and off-line processing.
User only task action	A type of task action which does not involve the use of the computer.
User/Computer task action	A type of task action which involves the use of the computer via the user-computer interface.
User Role	A collection of job holders who share a large proportion of common tasks or who have the same access security privileges for the system.
Window	A communication channel through which the user looks to view and interact with user objects.
Window Action	A manipulation of an element of a window which is used to implement a user object action.

8   PRODUCT DESCRIPTIONS FOR USER CENTRED DESIGN

Listed below are the Product Descriptions for those products produced during Work
Practice Modelling, User Object Modelling, (On-line) Function Definition, User Interface
Design and Prototyping and Evaluation. These Product Descriptions should not be
regarded as definitive, rather they are a start point that can be tailored for each individual
project. It is expected that each project will examine the composition list and add and
remove as necessary to suit their particular project. In addition, if a Case Tool is utilised
then the Case Tool may have a suggested list of its own.

8.1   Function Definition

Purpose

To describe units of processing which need to controlled as a whole in order to support users tasks. Function Definitions have several sub-purposes:

- to identify and define units of processing which need to be carried forward to physical design;

- to pull together products of analysis and design;

- to identify how to best organise the system processing to support the users' tasks which have been defined in Work Practice Modelling;

- to develop and confirm a common understanding between analyst and user of how the system processing is to be organised;

- to provide the basis for sizing and deriving design objectives.

Composition

Multiple function details each consisting of:

- Function Description;

- Function Navigation Model.

Position in System Development Template

Specification – External Design

Quality Criteria:

1   Is this a complete set of documentation for all identified functions?

2   Are the functions consistent with the description of tasks?

3   Are the functions logically defined with respect to identifying common function components?

4   For functions containing on-line elements, do all UOM attributes appear in at least one Function Definition?

5   Is there at least one Function Definition for each required task which needs automated support?

External Dependencies

None

8.2   Function Description

Purpose

To define a function which is to be provided by the required system to support a user's tasks. To provide a description of the function and cross-references to related products.

Suitability

Function Descriptions are suitable where the:

- size of the target domain is high;
- complexity of functions is high;
- formality of business processes is high.

Composition

Heading details:

- Function Name;
- Function Identifier;
- Function Type.

Function details:

- Function text;
- Potential Problems.

References to:

- Task or sub-task supported;
- User Roles;
- User Object Model components;
- Requirements Catalogue Entries;
- Related functions;
- Event details, repeating group consisting of:
  - event name/identifier;
  - event frequency.
- Enquiry details, repeating group consisting of:

- Enquiries;

- Enquiry Frequency.

- Volumes

- Service Level Requirements, repeating group of:

  - Service Level Description;

- Service Level Target Value;

- Service Level Range;

- Service Level Comments.

Position in System Development Template

Specification – External Design

Quality Criteria:

1   Is the Function Description complete in that all items that can be identified are present?

2   Is the function identifier unique?

3   Is the function specified with cross-references to the User Object Model and Required Task Models?

4   If this is an off-line function, does it cross-reference the Required System Data Flow Model and I/0 Structures?

5   Is the function classified according to all three types:

     - update or enquiry;

     - on-line or off-line;

     - user or system initiated?

External Dependencies

Relevant users to join the review team.

8.3   Function Navigation Model

Purpose

To show the navigation between function components and the main function processing.

Composition

A diagram consisting of:

- boxes representing either the controlling function processing or the processing of a function component;
- arrows indicating permitted navigation paths.

Position in System Development Template

Specification – External Design

Quality Criteria:

1   Does the diagram represent all function components correctly?

2   Does the navigation support the requirements of the user's task which is supported by this function?

3   Is the diagram consistent with the description of the function in the Function Description?

4   Can any of the function components be combined (if so they should be)?

8.3.1 External Dependencies

Users closely involved with validation.

8.4   Required Task Model

Purpose

The complete set of Required Task Models describes all of the human activities and task sequences required by the business system. The Required Task Models elaborate the tasks identified by the mapping of business activities onto the user Organisation. Required Task Models cover all of the main task areas and some of the less common tasks.

Composition

Task Model Structure

Task Descriptions

Position in System Development Template

User Organisation

Quality Criteria:

1   Is there comprehensive coverage of required tasks?

2   Have preconditions for performing a task been reduced to a minimum?

3   For each Required Task Model is there a clear task goal?

4   Is it clear what information is required to perform the task and what information is produced as a result?

External Dependencies

None.

8.5   Task Description

Purpose

Task Descriptions are the supporting documentation for the Task Models. They are textual descriptions of each task.

Composition

A Task Description is completed as background information to any task or sub-task considered to require further description.

Each Task Description includes the following (although this should not be regarded as a definitive list):

- triggering business event;
- task goal;
- actor/user role;
- frequency – how often it is performed;
- expected duration of task;
- context of the task;
- physical environment of the task;
- task preconditions;
- equipment used to perform the task;
- information required to perform the task (this is used to help in deriving user objects in the User Object Model – see Chapter 5).

Position in System Development Template

User Organisation

Quality Criteria:

For each:

1   Is the description of adequate detail?

2   Is the description consistent with the corresponding Required Task Model?

For the set:

3   Have all tasks been described?

External Dependencies

None.

8.6   Task Model Structure

Purpose

To represent a task in a diagrammatic format. A Task Model Structure represents a task and its sub-tasks as a hierarchy. To indicate valid sequences of sub-tasks to be used as an input to job design and User Interface Design.

Composition

Diagram elements representing:

- tasks and sub-tasks;

- lines which indicate decomposition;

- textual plans (the possible sequences of sub-tasks within a task or superior sub-task).

Position in System Development Template

User Organisation

Quality Criteria:

For each:

1   Is the chosen notation used consistently?

2   Do plans cover all possible sub-task sequences?

3   Are tasks decomposed to the level where human sub-tasks are distinguished from user/computer sub-tasks?

For the set:

4   Have all tasks been modelled?

External Dependencies

None.

8.7   Task Scenario

Purpose

To provide a concrete example of a specific path through a task. Each Task Scenario describes the actions that a user will perform in using the system to achieve a goal or respond to a business event. The Task Scenario is validated with users to gain an understanding of what the system is likely to need to cope with. Task Scenarios can be used for the following purposes:

- to validate subsequent design work;
- as an input to prototyping;
- to improve communication with users;
- the basis of user acceptance testing.

Composition

A textual description of the scenario including inputs, background and the way in which the tasks are performed. Sub-tasks performed by the system should be distinguished from sub-tasks performed by the user. It can be written in the form of a story or a script. The scenario should be annotated to indicate whether this is a typical scenario or likely to be an exception.

Position in System Development Template

User Organisation

Quality Criteria:

1   Is each scenario representative of real situations encountered by users?

2   Are the Task Scenarios consistent with the relevant Task Model?

3   Is sufficient information provided to ensure the Task Scenarios are understandable by the project team?

8.7.1 External Dependencies

None.

8.8   User Catalogue

Purpose

To provide a list of all on-line users of the required system and the tasks associated with them. This is used as input to the formation of user roles.

Composition

Each entry consists of:

- user/actor;
- task areas.

Position in System Development Template

User Organisation

Quality Criteria:

1   Are all user tasks identified for each user/actor?

2   Have all the necessary users/actors been investigated?

External Dependencies

Relevant users to review their entries in the User Catalogue.

8.9   User Class Descriptions

Purpose

To provide a description of characteristics and abilities of a section of the user population to determine the requirements for the style and general features of the user interface design. User Class Descriptions are optional products that would normally only be produced where there is a large and diverse user population. The information that is collected needs to be motivated by the design choices that are being considered.

Composition

Each user class can be described by one or more of the following properties (although this should not be regarded as a definitive list):

- type of user (direct/indirect/remote, etc.);
- experience level – both in the use of user interfaces and in the job (novice, intermediate, expert, etc.);
- frequency of use of the system (one hour a day, once a week, continuous, etc.) and length of time in job;
- whether the user has to use the system to do their job or can choose not to use it (mandatory/discretionary);
- education/intellectual abilities (typical qualifications held by members of the class, abilities required by tasks currently performed);
- motivation and the specific goals for using the system
- costs/ benefits of the new system to this user class, increase/ decrease in skills/ prestige, etc.);
- numbers of users in the user class;
- training received/required;
- tasks performed (cross-reference to Required Task Models);
- other tools/systems used in performing their jobs.

Position in System Development Template

User Organisation

Quality Criteria:

1   Is there sufficient information to guide analysis and design decisions?

2   Within each user class, are the characteristics and usability requirements similar? (If the system is usable by a few members of the user class who participate in acceptance testing, is it reasonable to infer that it will be usable by others?)

3   Have the numbers of users in each class been identified?

4   Have the benefits of using the system been identified for each user class?

5   Have the implications for use been made explicit for each user class?

8.9.1 External Dependencies

Relevant users to review User Class Descriptions.

8.10 User Interface Design

Purpose

To document the overall design of the interface between the user and automated application.

Composition

- Window Navigation Model
- Window Specifications
- Help System Specification

Position in System Development Template

Specification – External Design

Quality Criteria:

1   Is the overall design simple and flexible?

2   How well does the design support the tasks the user needs to perform?

3   Can the user interpret what the representation means easily and correctly, relate it to their tasks and understand any feedback they receive?

4   Does the design conform with the User Object Model?

5   Does the design conform with the Installation and Application Style Guides?

6   Does the design satisfy the agreed usability requirements?

7   Does the design contain all the required help?

8   Is the design implementable in the chosen GUI environment?

9   Has the User Interface Design been evaluated by users and confirmed to be appropriate through prototyping?

8.10.1 External Dependencies

Users closely involved with validation.

8.11 User Object Description

Purpose

To provide supporting documentation for each user object from the User Object Model.

Composition

The following is a list of the items that can make up the composition of the User Object Description:

- User object ID;

- User object name;

- User object text to describe the user object;

- for each action in the user object a brief description of the resulting;

- processing and/or change of state together with cross-references to UOM attributes and events/enquiries invoked by the action;

- a list of UOM attributes (used only where the collapsed notation used in the User Object Structure).

Position in System Development Template

Specification – External Design

Quality Criteria:

1   Is each object on the User Object Structure described?

2   Are all UOM attributes in the user object manipulated by at least one action in the user object?

3   Are all UOM attributes also documented in the Data Catalogue?

8.11.1 External Dependencies

Users closely involved with validation.

8.12 User Object Model

Purpose

The User Object Model identifies the information which should be presented at the user interface, what associations are important to users, and the rules and relationships that should be preserved at the user interface. It is needed to develop an effective Organisation of the user interface which makes it easy for the users to learn and control the system.

Composition

- User Object Structure
- User Object Descriptions

Position in System Development Template

Specification – External Design

Quality Criteria:

1   Does the User Object Model contain the user objects and actions required to support the Required Task Models?

2   Are the terms used in naming user objects, actions and UOM attributes ones which the user understands in the context of their working environments

3   Are the cross-references to the Required System Logical Data Model documented in the Data Catalogue?

4   Are all events and enquiries cross-referenced to at least one action (unless the invocation is by the system)?

External Dependencies

Users closely involved with validation.

8.13 User Object Structure

Purpose

To provide a pictorial representation of the User Object Model.

Composition

- Diagram containing user objects and their associations
- User objects described on the diagram by a name, actions and UOM attributes. (Actions and UOM attributes optional where collapsed notation used)

Position in System Development Template

Specification - External Design

Quality Criteria:

1 Are all the user objects included in the diagram?

2 Are all associations required to support user tasks included?

3 Are notations used correctly and consistently?

4 Are all user objects supported by User Object Descriptions?

External Dependencies

None.

8.14 User Roles

Purpose

To package all user roles in the system into a complete set. User roles are those actors who will require direct access to the automated system within the business system.

Composition

Each user role has the following details:

- user role name/identifier;

- task details – repeating group consisting of

  - actor/user name;

  - tasks.

Position in System Development Template

User Organisation

Quality Criteria:

For each:

1   Does the user role subsume users/actors which should, to avoid compromising security, be kept separate?

2   Are activities correctly identified for the associated actor/user?

For the set:

3   Is this a complete set of documentation for all identified user roles in the proposed system?

External Dependencies

None.

8.15 Work Practice Model

Purpose

To identify the best mapping of the user Organisation onto business activities defined in the Business Activity Model. To define in detail the tasks undertaken by actors. To identify the human elements of the business system and to ensure the new automated system fits within the context of the business requirements as a whole. To define user roles required for the new automated system.

Composition

Tasks mapped to actors and user roles (product for this not defined in detail)

Required Task Models

User Catalogue

User roles

User Class Descriptions

Position in System Development Template

User Organisation

Quality Criteria:

1   Have techniques been applied which ensure that the user Organisation mapping onto business activities has been optimised?

2   Are users able to identify with the tasks defined and the way in which they have been organised?

3   Does the Work Practice Model contain a clear demarcation between tasks which are human only and those which will require a user interface?

8.15.1 External Dependencies

None.

8.16 Window Navigation Model

Purpose

To represent the windows required to support the user interface and the navigation between them. A Window Navigation Model is concerned with how the user opens new windows and transfers focus from one window to another. The aim of developing the Window Navigation Model is to:

- ensure that the window structure supports the user tasks;

- check that window navigation is minimised and users don't have to switch between different dialog boxes to get the information they need;

- ensure task completion points match up with the overall window structure;

- identify common dialogue structures and handle them in a consistent way;

- ensure functionality is placed where it is needed;

- ensure that exit points are provided for all transactions so users can cancel a transaction or put it on hold.

Composition

A diagram consisting of:

- windows;

- window actions;

- arrows indicating transfer between windows.

Position in System Development Template

Specification –External Design

Quality Criteria:

1.   Are the windows defined consistent with the description of the function and Function Navigation Model?

2.   Are exit points explicit in the model?

3.   Are window types correctly used in the context of the navigation specified?

4   Has navigation been minimised – can windows be combined?

External Dependencies

Users closely involved with validation.

8.17 Window Specification

Purpose

A Window Specification is a detailed description of a window that will be used as the basis for the implementation of the window. Window Specifications can be developed at different levels of detail. For simple windows it is usually adequate to develop a rough hand-drawn sketch or prototype. For more complex, critical windows it is advised that a full specification is produced.

Composition

A detailed Window Specification should describe the following features:

- window display, preferably in the form of a picture showing a sketch or prototype window design;

- window type (modality, number of instances, whether it can be resized);

- window title bar including: Window menu, title or how generated and window icons and menus;

- actions prior to displaying the window such as identifying any context that needs to be set, populating lists and defaults that are set; control behaviour that needs to be defined. Such as:

  - type of list boxes, for example whether they will allow single or multiple selection, how they will be populated, the sort order to be used, the expected number of items in the box;

  - type of data entry fields, for example whether they are mandatory or optional, field length, validation, routines, defaults, format where these features have not already been recorded in the Data Catalogue.

- behaviour a window supports once it has been displayed. It is often better to define this using a prototype supported by a textual document that describes any additional features that are not demonstrated in the prototype;

- view description detailing any views that are shown within a dialogue box or window such as showing a form layout preview or a customer's previous contacts;

- messages generated from a dialog box can optionally be described together with tab sequences;

- help topic detailing the type of help and help on what. This might cross-reference the Help System Specification where appropriate;

- actions and behaviour that occur within the window or dialogue box which are not described in the Application Style Guide.

Position in System Development Template

Specification – External Design

Quality Criteria:

1   Is the window described to an appropriate level of detail?

2   Is the window consistent with the Window Navigation Model?

External Dependencies

Users closely involved with validation.

ANNEXE A – DESCRIPTION OF SYSTEM DEVELOPMENT TEMPLATE

The System Development Template (SDT) provides a common structure for the overall system development process. This template is used extensively in the definition of SSADM.

The System Development Template divides the development process into a number of distinct areas of concern, as shown in the diagram below.

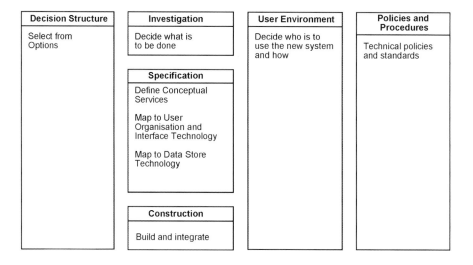

Figure A-1 System Development Template general view

The 3-schema specification architecture (which covers the Specification area) concentrates on those products that will ultimately lead, sometimes via other products, into elements of software. The SDT takes a broader view and divides the system development process into activity areas onto which all the development products may be mapped.

ANNEXE B – DESCRIPTION OF EU-RENT CASE STUDY

EU-Rent is a car rental company owned by EU-Corporation. It is one of three businesses – the other two being hotels and an airline – that each have their own business and IT systems, but share their customer base. Many of the car rental customers also fly with EU-Fly and stay at EU-Stay hotels.

EU-Rent business

EU-Rent has 1000 branches in towns all over Europe. At each branch cars, classified by car group, are available for rental. Each branch has a manager and booking clerks who handle rentals.

Rentals

Most rentals are by advance reservation; the rental period and the car group are specified at the time of reservation. EU-Rent will also accept immediate ('walk-in') rentals, if cars are available.

At the end of each day cars are assigned to reservations for the following day. If more cars have been requested than are available in a group at a branch, the branch manager may ask other branches if they have cars they can transfer to him/her.

Returns

Cars rented from one branch of EU-Rent may be returned to any other branch. The renting branch must ensure that the car has been returned to some branch at the end of the rental period. If a car is returned to a branch other than the one that rented it, ownership of the car is assigned to the new branch.

Servicing

EU-Rent also has service depots, each serving several branches. Cars may be booked for maintenance at any time provided that the service depot has capacity on the day in question.

For simplicity, only one booking per car per day is allowed. A rental or service may cover several days.

Customers

A customer can have several reservations but only one car rented at a time. EU-Rent keeps records of customers, their rentals and bad experiences such as late return, problems with payment and damage to cars. This information is used to decide whether to approve a rental.

Current IT system

Each branch and service depot has a local IT system based on PCs and a file server. The equipment is obsolete and limited in capacity (especially RAM). Hardware failures – screens, disk drives and power supplies – are increasingly frequent. There is currently no use of the Internet either for customer to business communication or for business to business communication.

Application maintainability

The application programs have been maintained over several years. Small RAM in the PCs has necessitated intricate, complex programs which makes amendments progressively more difficult and expensive.

Informal communication

Each location operates almost independently of others. Communication between locations is mainly by phone and fax and co-ordination is very variable. Sometimes, when a car is dropped off at a branch different from the pick-up branch, the drop-off branch will not inform the pick-up branch.

Branch managers tend to co-operate in small groups and not to look for 'spare' cars outside those groups. EU-Rent management feels that some capacity is wasted, but does not have reliable estimates of how much.

Scheduling of service bookings in branch and service depot files is co-ordinated by faxes between branch and depot. Sometimes service bookings are not recorded in the branch files, and cars booked for servicing are rented. Service depots sometimes do not get to know that a car has been transferred to a branch served by other depots until another depot requests the car's service history.

Customer blacklist

A copy of the customer blacklist is held at every branch. It should be updated every week from head office, but the logistics of updating the list with input from 1000 sources and sending out 1000 disks every week are beyond head office's capability. Updates are in fact sent out about every four weeks.

E-Commerce

There is no current use of e-commerce with customers having to phone or fax the individual offices to book cars for rental. This is causing problems in that some competitors have introduced facilities that enable customers to book and monitor their bookings over the Internet and it is thought that this is resulting in a loss of custom.

IT system replacement

EU-Rent management has decided that a new IT system is needed. It is expected whilst the basic operational activity is not expected to change significantly – locations and volume of rentals – it is expected that a number of 'online' systems (e.g. ordering of cars) will be implemented not necessarily as part of the initial role out but shortly thereafter. The new system is justified on three grounds:

- the current system cannot be kept going much longer;

- the perceived need to introduce some online system that can be accessed directly by customers over the Internet;

- better management of numbers of cars at branches and better co-ordination between branches is expected to increase utilisation of cars slightly – the same volume of business should be supportable with fewer cars. Each car ties up about 8,000 Euros in capital and loses about 3,000 Euros in depreciation, so significant savings are possible from small reductions in numbers of cars needed.

Corporate data

After the current IT system has been replaced, EU-Rent management wants to explore possibilities for sharing customer data across the car rental, hotel and airline systems. Even if customers are not stored in a single shared database, it makes sense for all three business areas to have consistent customer information on current address, telephone number, credit rating, etc.

It will be useful to know in each system when there are problems with a customer in other systems. And it may be possible to run promotions in one system, based on what EU-Corporation knows from the other systems about customers.

Future requirements

A customer loyalty incentive scheme is also under consideration. The requirement is not yet precisely defined but the scheme will be comparable with those offered by EU-Rent's competitors.

Members of the scheme will accumulate credit points with each car rental. They will exchange points for 'free' rentals. Only the base rental price will be payable by points; extra charges such as insurance and fuel will be paid for by cash or credit card. When this is introduced it is expected that customers will wish to be able to check (either by the use of a call-centre or directly over the Internet) the current state of their credit points.

Rationale for EU-Rent

The business of EU-Rent is car rentals, but this is largely irrelevant; it merely provides an easily understood context for examples. The business issues and user requirements in EU-Rent could be easily mapped to other systems. They include:

- a requirement to deliver a range of services (rental of cars of different quality and price) at many locations (rental branches), with different volumes of business and patterns of demand;

- customers who may use more than one location, but whose business with the whole organisation should be tracked;

- strong general policies set centrally (car models that may be used, rental tariffs, procedures for dealing with customers), but significant flexibility and authority for local managers (number of cars owned by branch, authority to over-ride published tariff to beat competitors' prices);

- a requirement for customers to be able to directly access aspects of the system;

- performance targets for local managers;

- a requirement for capacity planning and resource replenishment (disposal and purchase of cars, moving of cars between branches); possibilities for this to be managed locally, regionally or centrally;

- locally-managed sharing or swapping of resources or customers between branches to meet short-term unforeseen demand;

- an internal support structure (the maintenance depots) needed to maintain the resources and ensure that the product delivered to customers is of adequate quality;

- a customer base that is shared with other, separate systems (EU-Stay hotels and EU-Fly airline), and possibilities of communicating or co-ordinating with these systems.

Many of these characteristics are common to other types of business; for example, health care, vocational training, social security, policing, retail chain stores, branch banking.

ANNEXE C – GLOSSARY OF TERMS

Actor

A term used to identify a collection of proposed job holders who share a large proportion of common tasks, whether using the IT system or not.

Application Style Guide

Should be regarded as a set of standards, covering the user interface, to be followed within a particular application development. This document is based on the Installation Style Guide and tailored to the specific needs of a particular project.

Association

Is a relationship between two user objects, on a User Object Model, that the system will need to provide.

attribute

A characteristic property of an entity, or entity aspect, that is, any detail that serves to describe, qualify, identify, classify, quantify or express the state of an entity.

business activity

A transformation in the business system which acts on inputs to produce outputs. Business activities can be dependent on other business activities, they can be triggered by business events and are performed by actors in the business system. Business activities are the major components of a Business Activity Model. Where a business activity requires information support or is a candidate for automation, this will give rise to requirements in the Requirements Catalogue.

business event

A trigger to one or more business activities.

CASE tools

Computer-aided Software Engineering (CASE) tools are automated tools supporting analysts in their use of design techniques. This type of tool normally supports the diagrammatic techniques as well as containing a repository of information supporting the diagrams.

character-based interface

Character-based interfaces rely on the use of a character set which is displayed on the screen in a matrix of columns and rows. These character sets can include block graphic characters which allow simple boxes to be drawn.

enquiry

An element which requires information to be read from the Logical Data Model but involves no update processing. Some update functions contain enquiries as well as updates (events).

event

An event is something that triggers a Conceptual Model process to update the system data. It is usually sourced by an event which occurs in the business environment, notified to the system via one or more functions. An event provides the reason for an update process to be initiated. The name of the event should reflect what is causing the process to be invoked and not the process name itself. Typical event names might include terms such as 'Receipt', 'Notification', 'Decision', 'Arrival', 'New', 'Change' event data

function

A user-defined packaging of events and enquiries and the processing they trigger that will be accessed from the External Design. Functions can be categorised as enquiry/update, off-line/on-line, user-initiated/system initiated. This volume covers only on-line functions.

Function Definition (technique)

For on-line functions Function Definition identifies units of processing specification, or functions, which package together the essential services of the system in the way required by the user organisation.

Function Definition (product)

The product of the Function Definition technique is a group product called the Function Definition. This is composed of the following products:

- Function Description;

- Function Navigation Model.

Function Description

The Function Description contains some descriptive text and a large number of cross-references to other products. The precise format of the product will depend upon the documentation tools available to the project.

Function Navigation Model

A model, constructed for complex functions, which shows how the different parts of the function relate to each other.

Graphical User Interface (GUI)

Graphical User Interfaces (GUIs) allow each dot or pixel on the screen to be addressed individually. Characters are made up of groups of pixels and can be made any size and in a variety of fonts. Graphic objects such as lines and arcs can be drawn. GUIs are almost always used in conjunction with windows, icons, a mouse and pop-up or pull-down menus.

Help System Specification

A description of the help system in terms of the procedures to be adopted for help and areas to be covered.

Logical Data Model

Provides an accurate model of the information requirements of all or part of an organisation. This serves as a basis for file and database design, but is independent of any specific implementation technique or product.

menu

A hierarchical structure used to provide a user (role) with access to available, and applicable functions.

Menu Structure

Provides a diagrammatic representation of the menus to be used within the system.

off-line function

A function where all the data is input and the whole of the database processing for the function is completed without further interaction with the user.

on-line function

A function where the system and the user communicate through input and output messages, i.e., message pairs. The system responds in time to influence the next input message. On-line functions may include off-line elements such as printing an off-line report.

Product Description

Describes the purpose, form and components of a product, and lists the quality criteria which apply to it.

prototype

Provides the user with an animated view of how the system being developed will work. It enhances user understanding, allowing better identification of discrepancies and deficiencies in the user requirement. It can used as part of incremental development.

Requirements Catalogue

Is the central repository for information covering all identified requirements, both functional and non-functional. Each entry is textual and describes a required facility or feature of the proposed system.

Style Guide

A guide which shows how to implement various elements of the user interface. Style Guides are of great importance in projects to ensure a common look and feel across all the facilities within the application.

There are two main types of style guide:

- the Installation Style Guide, which sets broad standards for all applications within the organisation as a whole;

- the Application Style Guide, which is an elaboration of the Installation Style Guide for use on a particular project.

System Development Template

The System Development Template provides a common structure for the overall system development process.

It divides the process into a number of distinct areas of concern:

- Investigation;
- Specification;
- Construction;
- Decision Structure;
- User Organisation;
- Policies and Procedures.

task

A human activity performed by an actor in response to a business event. The task is identified, from the 'human' perspective, with reference to all the business activities triggered by a specific business event which are undertaken by a single actor.

Task Model

A model which describes all of the human activities and task sequences required by the business system. The Task Model elaborate the tasks identified by the mapping of business activities onto the user organisation. Task Models tend to cover all the major tasks and a subset of the less common tasks. Task Models are documented as part of the Work Practice Model.

User Catalogue

Provides a description of the on-line users of the proposed system. It includes details of job titles and the tasks undertaken by each of the identified users.

user

A person who will require direct interaction with the automated system.

user class

A subset of the total population of users of the required system who are similar in terms of their frequency of use, relevant knowledge and personal experience.

User Object

Something the user will want to recognise as a component of the user interface of the automated system. User Objects may represent a set of data, a computer system device or a container for other user objects. User Objects are modelled on the User Object Model.

User Object Model

A model made up of User Objects and Associations which is, in essence, a user's mental model of the structure and contents of the system. It would be usual to build a single User Object Model for the system which is used as a vital part of the design of the user interface.

user role

A collection of job holders who share a large proportion of common tasks or who have the same access security privileges for the system.

window

A communication channel through which the user looks to view and interact with elements of the automated system.

Window Navigation Model

A model which describes the window and dialogue structure and how the user navigates between windows.

Window Specifications

A specification which describes how the window will look in terns of views, states and actions. The specifications can be produced textually or as part of a prototype.

Work Practice Model

This is the mapping of business activities and scheduling constraints onto an Organisation Structure. This requires the definition of user roles and classification of users (derived from User Analysis) so that business activities can be assigned to 'actors'.

INDEX

Q

R